AIRFRAME & POWERPLANT MECHANICS

POWERPLANT WORKBOOK
Written, Oral, and Practical

ALIGNS WITH

FAA-H-8083-32B & FAA-H-8083-32B-ATB

Airframe & Powerplant Mechanics Powerplant Handbook

by Thomas Wild

Aircraft Technical Book Company
72413 US Hwy 40 - Tabernash, CO 80478-0270 USA
(970) 726-5111
www.actechbooks.com

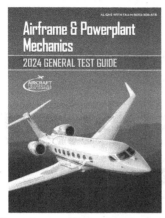

PREFACE

This Student Workbook is designed as a companion to the Aviation Maintenance Mechanics Powerplant Handbook FAA-H-8083-32 and FAA-H-8083-32B-ATB. Each chapter of this workbook matches the equivalent chapter in the Handbook and contains study questions, exercises, and a final exam for that chapter. Each is designed to enhance your understanding of the material in the textbook and to better prepare you for success with your actual FAA written exams and later in your career as a professional aviation maintenance technician.

Each chapter of this Workbook is presented in 3 parts:
1. Study Aid Questions are fill in the blank, multiple choice, true or false, or matching formats designed to reinforce the most important concepts presented in the Handbook.
2. Knowledge Application Questions; giving you an opportunity to actually use the material presented in each chapter to solve common problems.
3. Final Chapter Exam, in multiple choice format designed to further reinforce your study skills and to be used by instructors as end of chapter exam and as an evaluation of your progress.

The answers to Sections A&B questions may be found in the back of this workbook and can so be used by students as a part of your personal study habits. The answers to Section C - Final Chapter Exams, are available only to instructors as part of the instructor support package for the H-8083 textbook series, thus preserving the value of the exam as a valid instructional tool.

Each page in this book is perforated allowing students to tear out and turn in assigned sections which may be given as homework or in-class exercises.

For further information about this Workbook, its corresponding Textbook, or to order additional copies in print or electronic format, please contact Aircraft Technical Book Company at (970) 726-5111, or email to orders@actechbooks.com, or visit our web site at www.actechbooks.com.

TABLE OF CONTENTS

ISBN: 978-1951275815

9 781951 275815

PAGE LEFT BLANK INTENTIONALLY

AIRCRAFT ENGINES

CHAPTER 1

Study Aid Questions - Fill In The Blanks

1. _____ is the principal fluid used for propulsion in every type of aircraft powerplant except the _____ .

2. Specific fuel consumption for gas turbines is the _____ measured in _____ / _____ divided by (lbs.); and for reciprocating engines it is the fuel flow (lbs./hr.) divided by _____ .

3. The foundation of an engine is the _____ .

4. _____ in an engine not only results in fatigue failure of the metal structures, but also causes the moving parts to _____ .

5. The purpose of the _____ rings are to prevent the escape of combustion gases past the piston during engine operation.

6. What are the three major types of propeller shafts?
   _____ , _____ , _____ .

7. The physicist defines work as; work is _____ times _____ .

8. _____ can be considered as the result of the engine and the propeller working together.

9. A significant feature of gas turbine engines is that separate sections are devoted to each _____ and all functions are performed _____ without interruption.

10. The Indicated Mean Effective Pressure (IMEP), is the _____ produced in the _____ during the operating cycle and is an expression of the theoretical, frictionless power known as _____ .

11. Volumetric efficiency is a ratio expressed in terms of _____ .

12. Volumetric efficiency is a comparison of the volume of fuel/air charge (corrected for temperature and pressure), inducted into the _____ to the _____ .

13. The standard sea level temperature is _____ or _____ . At this temperature the pressure of one atmosphere is _____ lbs/sq-inch. This pressure will support a column of mercury _____ inches high.

14. Four types of gas turbine engines are used to propel and power aircraft, are
    _____ , _____ , _____ , _____ .

15. The two principal types of compressors currently being used in gas turbine aircraft engines are
    _____ , _____ .

AIRCRAFT ENGINES

_____ 1. The centrifugal-flow compressor consists basically of an impeller (rotor), a diffuser (stator), and a compressor manifold.

_____ 2. The centrifugal-flow compressor has two main elements, a rotor and a stator.

_____ 3. The diffuser is the divergent section of the engine after the compressor and before the combustion section.

_____ 4. The combustion section houses the combustion process, which raises the temperature of the air passing through the engine.

_____ 5. The primary function of the combustion section is to burn the fuel/air mixture, thereby removing heat energy from the air and transferring it to the engine.

_____ 6. A very important requirement in the construction of combustion chambers is providing the means for draining unburned fuel which prevents gum deposits in the fuel manifold, nozzles, and combustion chambers.

_____ 7. The turbine transforms a portion of the kinetic (velocity) energy of the exhaust gases into mechanical energy to drive the gas generator compressor and accessories.

_____ 8. After the combustion chamber has introduced the heat energy into the mass airflow and delivered it evenly to the turbine inlet nozzles, it becomes the job of the nozzles to prepare the mass air flow for driving the compressor rotor.

_____ 9. The turbine wheel is a dynamically balanced unit consisting of blades attached to a rotating disk.

_____ 10. Many turbine blades are cast as a single crystal which gives the blades better strength and heat properties.

_____ 11. A turbine stage consists of a row of stationary vanes or nozzles, followed by a row of rotating blades.

_____ 12. The minimum number of bearings required to support one shaft is two deep groove ball bearing (thrust and radial loads) and four straight roller bearing (radial load only).

Section A
Matching

Which of the following components are associated with a Reciprocating Engine Cylinder. Answers can be in any order.

A. Exhaust Valve   E. Camshaft   I. Push Rods   M. Valve Springs
B. Connecting Rod   F. Intake Valve   J. Piston   N. Valve Guides
C. Crankshaft   G. Rocker Arm Shaft   K. Crankcase   O. Turbine
D. Valve Seats   H. Rocker Arm   L. Compressor

1. _____   3. _____   5. _____   7. _____   9. _____

2. _____   4. _____   6. _____   8. _____   10. _____

Section B
Knowledge Application Questions

1. Aircraft using propellers create thrust by?

2. What is the purpose of the piston compression rings?

3. Describe an opposed type of reciprocating engine.

4. Explain the operation of hydraulic valve lifters/tappets.

5. What is the formula for calculating indicated horsepower?

6. List the typical sections that a gas turbine engines consist of.

7. What is the formula for determining force or thrust developed by a gas turbine engine?

8. Describe thermal efficiency.

9. What methods are used with turbine blades and inlet guide vanes to increase the exhaust temperatures entering the turbine section of the engine?

10. Describe centrifugal-flow compressor components, pressure rise, and limits.

Chapter 1, Section B - Aircraft Engines

Name:_____ Date:_____

PAGE LEFT BLANK INTENTIONALLY

Section C
Final Chapter Exam

1. On which strokes are both valves on a four-stroke cycle reciprocating aircraft engine open?
   ☐ A. Power and exhaust.
   ☐ B. Intake and compression.
   ☐ C. Exhaust and intake.

2. Which statement is true regarding bearings used in high powered reciprocating aircraft engines?
   ☐ A. The outer race of a single row, self aligning ball bearing will always have a radius equal to the radius of the balls.
   ☐ B. There is less rolling friction when ball bearings are used than when roller bearings are employed.
   ☐ C. Crankshaft bearings are generally of the ball-type due to their ability to withstand extreme loads without overheating.

3. Master rod bearings are generally what type?
   ☐ A. Plain
   ☐ B. Roller
   ☐ C. Ball

4. A nine cylinder engine with a bore of 5.5 inches and a stroke of 6 inches will have a total piston displacement of _____
   ☐ A. 740 cubic inches.
   ☐ B. 1,425 cubic inches.
   ☐ C. 1,283 cubic inches.

5. Which statement is correct regarding engine crankshafts?
   ☐ A. Movable counterweights serve to reduce the dynamic vibrations in an aircraft reciprocating engine.
   ☐ B. Movable counterweights serve to reduce the torsional vibrations in an aircraft reciprocating engine.
   ☐ C. Movable counterweights are designed to resonate at the natural frequency of the crankshaft.

6. If fuel/air ratio is proper and ignition timing is correct, the combustion process should be completed?
   ☐ A. 20 to 30° before top center at the end of the compression stroke.
   ☐ B. When the exhaust valve opens at the end of the power stroke.
   ☐ C. Just after top center at the beginning of the power stroke.

7. The primary concern in establishing the firing order for an opposed engine is to _____
   ☐ A. provide for balance and eliminate vibration to the greatest extent possible.
   ☐ B. keep power impulses on adjacent cylinders as far apart as possible in order to obtain the greatest mechanical efficiency.
   ☐ C. keep the power impulses on adjacent cylinders as close as possible in order to obtain the greatest mechanical efficiency.

8. The five events of a four-stroke cycle engine in the order of their occurrence are _____
   ☐ A. intake, ignition, compression, power, exhaust.
   ☐ B. intake, power, compression, ignition, exhaust.
   ☐ C. intake, compression, ignition, power, exhaust.

9. Which bearing is least likely to be a roller or ball bearing?
   ☐ A. Rocker arm bearing (overhead valve engine).
   ☐ B. Master rod bearing (radial engine).
   ☐ C. Crankshaft main bearing (radial engine).

10. Which of the following is a characteristic of a thrust bearing used in most radial engines?
    ☐ A. Tapered roller.
    ☐ B. Double row ball.
    ☐ C. Deep groove ball.

AIRCRAFT ENGINES

11. Which of the following will decrease volumetric efficiency in a reciprocating engine?
    01. Full throttle operation.
    02. Low cylinder head temperatures.
    03. Improper valve timing.
    04. Sharp bends in the induction system.
    05. High carburetor air temperatures.
    - ☐ A. 02, 04, and 05
    - ☐ B. 01, 02, 03, and 04
    - ☐ C. 03, 04, and 05

12. The valve clearance of an engine using hydraulic lifters, when the lifters are completely flat, or empty, should not exceed _____
    - ☐ A. 0.00 inch
    - ☐ B. a specified amount above zero.
    - ☐ C. a specified amount below zero.

13. The actual power delivered to the propeller of an aircraft engine is called _____
    - ☐ A. friction horsepower.
    - ☐ B. brake horsepower.
    - ☐ C. indicated horsepower.

14. What is the principal advantage of using propeller reduction gears?
    - ☐ A. To enable the propeller RPM to be increased without an accompanying increase in engine RPM.
    - ☐ B. To enable the engine RPM to be increased with an accompanying increase in power and allow the propeller to remain at a lower, more efficient RPM.
    - ☐ C. To enable the engine RPM to be increased with an accompanying increase in propeller RPM.

15. The horsepower developed in the cylinders of a reciprocating engine is known as the _____
    - ☐ A. shaft horsepower.
    - ☐ B. indicated horsepower.
    - ☐ C. brake horsepower.

16. Cam ground pistons are installed in some aircraft engines to _____
    - ☐ A. provide a better fit at operating temperatures.
    - ☐ B. act as a compensating feature so that a compensated magneto is not required.
    - ☐ C. equalize the wear on all pistons.

17. What does valve overlap promote?
    - ☐ A. Lower intake manifold pressure and temperatures.
    - ☐ B. A backflow of gases across the cylinder.
    - ☐ C. Better scavenging and cooling characteristics.

18. Excessive valve clearance in a piston engine _____
    - ☐ A. increases valve overlap.
    - ☐ B. increases valve opening time.
    - ☐ C. decreases valve overlap.

19. When does valve overlap occur in the operation of an aircraft reciprocating engine?
    - ☐ A. At the end of the exhaust stroke and the beginning of the intake stroke.
    - ☐ B. At the end of the power stroke and the beginning of the exhaust stroke.
    - ☐ C. At the end of the compression stroke and the beginning of the power stroke.

20. The primary purpose in setting proper valve timing and overlap is _____
    - ☐ A. permit the best possible charge of fuel/air mixture into the cylinders.
    - ☐ B. gain more thorough exhaust gas scavenging.
    - ☐ C. obtain the best volumetric efficiency and lower cylinder operating temperatures.

21. The volume of a cylinder equals 70 cubic inches when the piston is at bottom center. When the piston is at the top of the cylinder, the volume equals 10 cubic inches. What is the compression ratio?
    ☐ A. 1:7
    ☐ B. 7:10
    ☐ C. 7:1

22. The basic gas turbine engine is divided into two main sections: the cold section and the hot section.
    01. The cold section includes the engine inlet, compressor, and turbine sections.
    02. The hot section includes the combustor, diffuser, and exhaust sections.
    Regarding the above statements,
    ☐ A. Only No. 01 is true.
    ☐ B. Only No. 02 is true.
    ☐ C. Neither No. 01 or No. 02 are true.

23. A turbine engine compressor which contains vanes on both sides of the impeller is a _____
    ☐ A. double entry centrifugal compressor.
    ☐ B. double entry axial flow compressor.
    ☐ C. single entry axial flow compressor.

24. What are the two functional elements in a centrifugal compressor?
    ☐ A. Turbine and compressor.
    ☐ B. Bucket and expander.
    ☐ C. Impeller and diffuser.

25. What is the purpose of the diffuser section in a turbine engine?
    ☐ A. To increase pressure and reduce velocity.
    ☐ B. To convert pressure to velocity.
    ☐ C. To reduce pressure and increase velocity.

Chapter 1, Final Chapter Exam - Aircraft Engines

Name:_____   Date:_____

PAGE LEFT BLANK INTENTIONALLY

ENGINE AND FUEL METERING SYSTEMS

Section A
Study Aid Questions - Fill In The Blanks

1. The engine fuel system must supply _____ to the engine's _____ under all conditions of ground and air operation.

2. The most common fuel is _____ for reciprocating engines and _____ turbine engines.

3. Avgas is generally colored to identify its type. 80 octane avgas is colored _____ 100LL avgas is colored _____ .

4. Gas turbine fuel controls have greatly improved the ability to _____ the fuel correctly during all flight regimes.

5. The LL in 100LL avgas stands for _____ though it contains 4 times the _____ of 80 octane avgas.

6. By the use of _____ and _____ built in to electronic controls, the engines can be controlled with much more accuracy.

7. Many engines use an interactive system that senses engine _____ and feeds the information to the _____ (electronic engine control).

8. _____ fuel temperatures often combine with _____ pressure to increase vapor formation.

9. _____ can become serious enough to block the fuel flow completely and stop the engine.

10. Due to the atmospheric pressure _____ as altitude is _____ the density of the air will also decrease.

ENGINE AND FUEL METERING SYSTEMS

11. There is less danger of _____ , since the drop in temperature due to fuel _____ takes place in or near the cylinder.

12. _____ is also improved because of the positive action of the fuel-injection system.

13. The fuel-injection system also gives greater _____ than a system in which the mixture to most cylinders must be _____ than necessary so that the cylinder with the leanest mixture will operate properly.

14. The fuel discharge nozzle is located in the _____ with its outlet directed into the _____ .

15. The fuel nozzles form part of the turbine engine fuel system and _____ or _____ the fuel so that it will ignite and burn efficiently.

Section A
True of False

_____ 1. Less air flow entering the carburetor will tend to make carburetors run richer at altitude than at ground level.

_____ 2. It is necessary that a mixture control be provided to lean the mixture and compensate for increased altitude.

_____ 3. If an engine is operating at high power setting with a very lean mixture, the cylinder head temperatures would exceed the maximum permissible temperatures and detonation would occur.

_____ 4. Gasoline and other liquid fuels will burn even if they are not mixed with air.

_____ 5. A mixture with a ratio of 12 to 1 (12:1) is made up of 12 lbs. of air and 1 lb. of fuel.

_____ 6. The stoichiometric mixture produces the lowest combustion temperatures because the proportion of heat released to a mass of charge (fuel and air) is the greatest.

_____ 7. An engine running near full power requires a very lean mixture to prevent overheating and detonation.

_____ 8. As the air speeds up to get through the narrow portion of a venturi, its pressure drops.

_____ 9. The float operated needle valve, in a float carburetor, regulates the flow through the inlet which maintains the correct level in the fuel float chamber.

_____ 10. The discharge nozzle is located in the throat of the venturi at the point where the highest increase in pressure occurs as air passes through the carburetor to the engine cylinders.

_____ 11. If the throttle is moved toward the "closed" position, the airflow and fuel flow increase.

_____ 12. A carburetor's main metering system supplies fuel to the engine at all speeds above idle.

True of False (continued)

_____ 13. The mixture control system determines the ratio of fuel to air in the mixture.

_____ 14. A pressure-type carburetor discharges fuel into the air stream at a pressure well below atmospheric pressure.

_____ 15. Fuel evaporation ice or refrigeration ice is formed because of the decrease in air temperature resulting from the evaporation of fuel after it is introduced into the airstream.

Matching

Identify each component in the drawing below with the following terms:

Needle Valve	Main Metering Jet	Float Chamber	Idling System	Pump
Economizer	Float	Main Air Bleed	Fuel Inlet Screen	Main Discharge
Throttle Valve	Mixture Control	Venturi	Accelerating	Nozzle

Float-type Carburetor

1. _____   5. _____   9. _____   13. _____

2. _____   6. _____   10. _____   11. _____

3. _____   7. _____   11. _____

4. _____   8. _____   12. _____

Chapter 2, Section A - Engine and Fuel Metering Systems

Name:_____   Date:_____

PAGE LEFT BLANK INTENTIONALLY

Section B
Knowledge Application Questions

1. Explain the cause of vapor lock in fuel lines.

2. Describe the basic components that make up a typical fuel system.

3. What is the basic requirement of the reciprocating fuel metering system?

4. What is used to measure the air flow into the engine?

5. What is the function of the fuel mixture control in the fuel metering device?

6. How is fuel evaporation or refrigeration ice formed in the carburetor?

7. How is the fuel level in a float carburetor held at a fairly constant level?

8. What are some advantages of a fuel-injection system over a conventional carburetor system?

9. Explain the procedure for rigging the throttle cables.

10. What is the result of excessive rich or lean idle mixtures?

Chapter 2, Section B - Engine and Fuel Metering Systems

Name:_____   Date:_____

PAGE LEFT BLANK INTENTIONALLY

Section C
Final Chapter Exam

1. The fuel flow meter used with a continuous fuel-injection system installed on an aircraft's horizontally opposed reciprocating engine measures the fuel pressure drop across the _____
   - ☐ A. manifold valve.
   - ☐ B. fuel nozzles.
   - ☐ C. metering valve.

2. What are the positions of the pressurization valve and the dump valve in a jet engine fuel system when the engine is shut down?
   - ☐ A. Pressurization valve closed, dump valve open.
   - ☐ B. Pressurization valve open, dump valve open.
   - ☐ C. Pressurization valve closed, dump valve closed.

3. The economizer system in a float-type carburetor _____
   - ☐ A. keeps the fuel/air ratio constant.
   - ☐ B. functions only at cruise and idle speeds.
   - ☐ C. increases the fuel/air ratio at high power settings.

4. The primary purpose of the air bleed openings used with continuous flow fuel-injector nozzles is to _____
   - ☐ A. provide for automatic mixture control.
   - ☐ B. lean out the mixture.
   - ☐ C. aid in proper fuel vaporization.

5. Which type of fuel control is used on most of today's turbine engines?
   - ☐ A. Electromechanical.
   - ☐ B. Mechanical.
   - ☐ C. Hydromechanical or electronic.

6. The density of air is very important when mixing fuel and air to obtain a correct fuel to air ratio. Which of the following weighs the most?
   - ☐ A. 75 parts of dry air and 25 parts of water vapor.
   - ☐ B. 100 parts of dry air.
   - ☐ C. 50 parts of dry air and 50 parts of water vapor.

7. What effect does high atmospheric humidity have on the operation of a jet engine?
   - ☐ A. Decreases engine pressure ratio.
   - ☐ B. Decreases compressor and turbine RPM.
   - ☐ C. Has little or no effect.

8. What carburetor component measures the amount of air delivered to the engine?
   - ☐ A. Economizer valve.
   - ☐ B. Automatic mixture control.
   - ☐ C. Venturi.

9. An aircraft carburetor is equipped with a mixture control in order to prevent the mixture from becoming too _____
   - ☐ A. lean at high altitudes.
   - ☐ B. rich at high altitudes.
   - ☐ C. rich at high speeds.

10. Why must a float-type carburetor supply a rich mixture during idle?
    - ☐ A. Engine operation at idle results in higher than normal volumetric efficiency.
    - ☐ B. At idling speeds the engine may not have enough airflow around the cylinders to provide proper cooling.
    - ☐ C. Because of reduced mechanical efficiency during idle.

ENGINE AND FUEL METERING SYSTEMS

11. Fuel is discharged for idling speeds on a float-type carburetor _____
    - ☐ A. from the idle discharge nozzle.
    - ☐ B. in the venturi.
    - ☐ C. through the idle discharge air bleed.

12. Which method is commonly used to adjust the level of a float in a float-type carburetor?
    - ☐ A. Lengthening or shortening the float shaft.
    - ☐ B. Add or remove shims under the needle valve seat.
    - ☐ C. Change the angle of the float arm pivot.

13. If an engine is equipped with a float-type carburetor and the engine runs excessively rich at full throttle the cause may be a(n) _____
    - ☐ A. main air bleed.
    - ☐ B. back suction line.
    - ☐ C. atmospheric vent line.

14. What is the possible cause of an engine running rich at full throttle if it is equipped with a float-type carburetor?
    - ☐ A. Float level too low.
    - ☐ B. Clogged main air bleed.
    - ☐ C. Clogged atmospheric vent.

15. What is a function of the idling air bleed in a float-type carburetor?
    - ☐ A. It provides a means for adjusting the mixture at idle speeds.
    - ☐ B. It vaporizes the fuel at idling speeds.
    - ☐ C. It aids in emulsifying/vaporizing the fuel at idle speeds.

16. On a carburetor without an automatic mixture control as you ascend to altitude, the mixture will _____
    - ☐ A. be enriched.
    - ☐ B. be leaned.
    - ☐ C. not be affected.

17. What are the principal advantages of the duplex fuel nozzle used in many turbine engines?
    - ☐ A. Restricts the amount of fuel flow to a level where more efficient and complete burning of the fuel is achieved.
    - ☐ B. Provides better atomization and uniform flow pattern.
    - ☐ C. Allows a wider range of fuels and filters to be used.

18. Kerosene is used as turbine engine fuel because _____
    - ☐ A. kerosene has very high volatility which aids in ignition and lubrication.
    - ☐ B. kerosene has more heat energy per gallon and lubricates fuel system components.
    - ☐ C. kerosene does not contain any water.

19. A method commonly used to prevent carburetor icing is _____
    - ☐ A. preheat the intake air.
    - ☐ B. mix alcohol with the fuel.
    - ☐ C. electrically heat the venturi and throttle valve.

20. If a fire starts in the induction system during the engine starting procedure, what should the operator do?
    - ☐ A. Turn off the fuel switches to stop the fuel.
    - ☐ B. Continue cranking the engine.
    - ☐ C. Turn off all switches.

21. The primary condition(s) that allow(s) microorganisms to grow in the fuel in aircraft fuel tanks are _____
    - ☐ A. warm temperatures and frequent fueling.
    - ☐ B. presence of water.
    - ☐ C. presence of dirt or other particulate contaminants.

22. What is added to aviation fuel to improve its antiknock qualities?
    ☐ A. Nitro.
    ☐ B. Lead.
    ☐ C. Diesel fuel.

23. During engine operation, if carburetor heat is applied, it will _____
    ☐ A. increase fuel/air ratio.
    ☐ B. increase engine RPM.
    ☐ C. decrease the air density to the carburetor.

24. What carburetor component limits the maximum airflow into the engine at full throttle?
    ☐ A. Throttle valve.
    ☐ B. Venturi.
    ☐ C. Main metering jet.

25. At what engine speed does the main metering jet actually function as a metering jet in a float-type carburetor?
    ☐ A. All RPM's.
    ☐ B. Cruising RPM only.
    ☐ C. All RPM's above idle range.

PAGE LEFT BLANK INTENTIONALLY

INDUCTION AND EXHAUST SYSTEMS

Section A
Study Aid Questions - Fill In The Blanks

1. The basic induction system of an aircraft reciprocating engine consists of an _____ used to collect the inlet air and ducting that transfers the air to the _____ .

2. The _____ prevents _____ and other _____ from entering the engine.

3. Induction systems can have different arrangement, they are the _____ and _____ type induction system.

4. Induction system ice can be prevented or eliminated by raising the _____ of the air that passes through the system, using a carburetor _____ system located upstream near the induction system inlet and well ahead of the _____ .

5. Throttle ice or any ice that restricts _____ or reduces _____ can best be removed by using full carburetor heat.

6. Ice can form in the induction system while an aircraft is flying in _____ , _____ , _____ , _____ , _____ , or even _____ that has high moisture content (high humidity).

7. The induction system should be checked for _____ and _____ during all regularly scheduled engine inspections. The units of the system should be checked for _____ .

8. A true _____ engine can boost the manifold pressure above _____ inches of mercury and are called _____ engines.

9. The temperature of the charge must be warm enough to ensure complete _____ and, thus, even distribution; but at the same time it must not be so _____ that it reduces _____ or causes _____ .

10. Externally driven superchargers derive their power from the energy of engine _____ directed against a _____ that drives an _____ that compresses the incoming air.

11. The compressor assembly of a turbo supercharger is made up of an _____ , a _____ , and a _____ .

12. If the waste gate is completely closed, all the exhaust gases are _____ and forced through the _____ .

13. When the waste gate is _____ , nearly all of the exhaust gases pass _____ providing little or no boost.

INDUCTION AND EXHAUST SYSTEMS

14. Almost all turbocharger systems use _____ as the control fluid for controlling the amount of boost (extra manifold pressure) provided to the engine.

15. The position of the waste gate is controlled by adjusting the _____ in the waste gate actuator.

16. The density controller is designed to limit the manifold pressure below the turbocharger's _____ and regulates bleed oil only at the _____ position.

17. The _____ functions during all positions of the waste gate valve other than the "fully open" position.

18. Many turbine engines use _____ to help straighten the air flow and direct it into the first stages of the compressor.

19. Engines that incorporate _____ as turboprops and APUs are not as vulnerable to _____.

20. The bellmouth is attached to the movable part of the _____ and _____ with the engine.

Section A
True or False

_____ 1. High bypass turbofan engines are usually constructed with the fan at the forward end of the compressor.

_____ 2. The air accelerated by the outer part of the fan blades forms a secondary airstream which is ducted overboard without passing through the main engine. This secondary air (fan flow) produces 20% of the thrust in high bypass engines.

_____ 3. There are two general types of exhaust systems in use on reciprocating aircraft engines: the long stack (closed) system and the connector system.

_____ 4. Although the collector system raises the back pressure of the exhaust, the gain in horsepower from turbo supercharging more than offsets the loss in horsepower from increased back pressure.

_____ 5. The augmenters are designed to produce a venturi effect to draw an increased airflow over the engine to augment engine cooling.

_____ 6. Exhaust system parts should never be marked with a lead pencil.

_____ 7. A good exhaust gasket seal is indicated by a flat gray or a sooty black streak on the pipes in the area of the sealed area.

_____ 8. Daily inspection of the exhaust system usually consists of checking the exposed exhaust system for cracks, scaling, excessive leakage, and loose clamps.

_____ 9. Any exhaust system failure should be regarded as a severe hazard.

_____ 10. Approximately half of all muffler and heat exchanger failures can be traced to cracks or ruptures in the heat exchanger surfaces used for cabin and carburetor heat sources.

_____ 11. Internal muffler failures (baffles, diffusers, etc.) are rarely cause for partial or complete engine power loss by restricting the flow of the exhaust gases.

True or False (continued)

_____ 12. When a turbocharger or a turbo supercharger system is included, the engine exhaust system operates under decreased pressure and temperature conditions.

_____ 13. Cracks in augmenter tubes can present a fire or carbon monoxide hazard by allowing exhaust gases to enter the nacelle, wing, or cabin areas.

_____ 14. Turboprop exhaust nozzles provide small amounts of thrust (10-15%) but are mainly used to discharge the exhaust gases from the aircraft.

_____ 15. The very first part of the exhaust nozzle and the exhaust plug form a convergent duct to reduce turbulence in the air flow.

Matching

Identify the items on the diagram:

1. _____   4. _____   7. _____

2. _____   5. _____   8. _____

3. _____   6. _____   9. _____

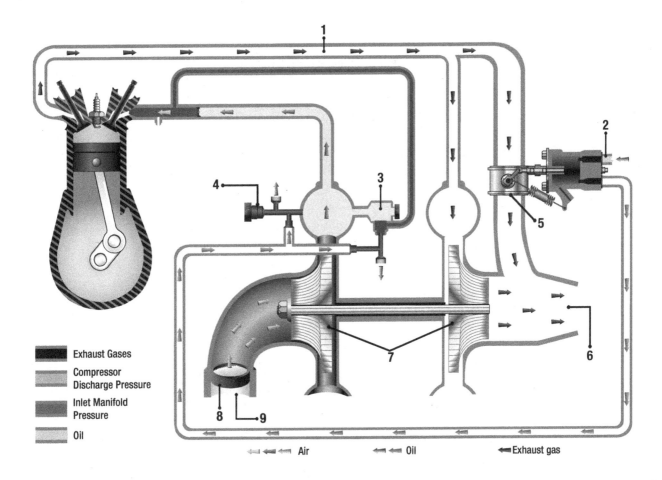

Chapter 3, Section A - Induction and Exhaust Systems

Name:_____   Date:_____

PAGE LEFT BLANK INTENTIONALLY

Section B
Knowledge Application Questions

1. Explain the basic operation of a down draft balanced induction system.

2. How can induction system icing be prevented or eliminated?

3. Why does part-throttle operation lead to an icing threat in the throttle area?

4. Describe a true supercharged engine.

5. What is the source of power for driving an external supercharger?

6. What controls the output of a typical turbocharger?

7. Explain the operation of the density controller.

8. When does the differential pressure controller function?

9. Explain the term "ram recovery" as it pertains to turbine engine intakes.

10. What is meant by the term "choked turbine exhaust nozzle"?

Chapter 3, Section B - Induction and Exhaust Systems

Name:_____ Date:_____

PAGE LEFT BLANK INTENTIONALLY

Section C
Final Chapter Exam

1. When will small induction system air leaks have the most noticeable effect on engine operation?
   - ☐ A. At high RPM.
   - ☐ B. At maximum continuous and takeoff power settings.
   - ☐ C. At low RPM.

2. A non-supercharged aircraft reciprocating engine operated at full throttle from sea level to 10,000 feet, provided the RPM is unchanged, will _____
   - ☐ A. lose power due to the reduced volume of air drawn into the cylinders.
   - ☐ B. produce constant power due to the same volume of air drawn into the cylinders.
   - ☐ C. lose power due to the reduced density of the air drawn into the cylinders.

3. An exhaust cone placed aft of the turbine in a jet engine will cause the pressure in the first part of the exhaust duct to _____
   - ☐ A. increase and the velocity to decrease.
   - ☐ B. increase and the velocity to increase.
   - ☐ C. decrease and the velocity to increase.

4. The velocity of supersonic air as it flows through a divergent nozzle does what?
   - ☐ A. Increases.
   - ☐ B. Decreases.
   - ☐ C. Is inversely proportional to the temperature.

5. The pressure of supersonic air as it flows through a divergent nozzle does what?
   - ☐ A. Increases.
   - ☐ B. Decreases.
   - ☐ C. Is inversely proportional to the temperature.

6. The pressure of subsonic air as it flows through a convergent nozzle does what?
   - ☐ A. Increases.
   - ☐ B. Decreases.
   - ☐ C. Is inversely proportional to the temperature.

7. The recurrent ingestion of dust or other fine airborne particulates into a turbine engine can result in _____
   - ☐ A. foreign object damage to the compressor section.
   - ☐ B. the need for less frequent abrasive grit cleaning of the engine.
   - ☐ C. erosion damage to the compressor and turbine sections.

8. The exhaust section of a turbine engine is designed to _____
   - ☐ A. impart a high exit velocity to the exhaust gases.
   - ☐ B. increase temperature, therefore increasing velocity.
   - ☐ C. decrease temperature, therefore decreasing pressure.

9. During inspection, hot section turbine engine components exposed to high temperatures may only be marked with such materials as allowed by the manufacturer. These materials generally include:

01. Layout Dye	03. Wax or Grease Pencil	05. Graphite Lead Pencil
02. Commercial Felt Tip Marker	04. Chalk	

   - ☐ A. 01, 02, and 04
   - ☐ B. 01, 03, and 04
   - ☐ C. 02, 04, and 05

10. The pressure of subsonic air as it flows through a convergent nozzle does what?
   - ☐ A. Increases.
   - ☐ B. Decreases.
   - ☐ C. Remains constant.

INDUCTION AND EXHAUST SYSTEMS

11. An indication of unregulated power changes that result in continual drift of manifold pressure indication on a turbo supercharged aircraft engine is known as _____
    - ☐ A. overshoot.
    - ☐ B. waste gate fluctuation.
    - ☐ C. bootstrapping.

12. What turbocharger controller controls the systems boost at full throttle?
    - ☐ A. Density controller.
    - ☐ B. Differential pressure controller.
    - ☐ C. Bootstrap valve.

13. The waste gate controls the flow of exhaust gases through the _____
    - ☐ A. compressor wheel assembly.
    - ☐ B. impeller.
    - ☐ C. turbine wheel assembly.

14. Turboprop air inlets are anti-iced using _____
    - ☐ A. electrical elements.
    - ☐ B. wire screens.
    - ☐ C. heat from the muffler.

15. A method commonly used to prevent carburetor icing is to _____
    - ☐ A. preheat the intake air.
    - ☐ B. mix alcohol with the fuel.
    - ☐ C. electrically heat the throttle valve.

16. What part of an aircraft in flight will begin to accumulate ice before any other?
    - ☐ A. Wing leading edge.
    - ☐ B. Propeller spinner or dome.
    - ☐ C. Carburetor.

17. Carburetor icing may be eliminated by which of the following methods?
    - ☐ A. Alcohol spray and electrically heated induction duct.
    - ☐ B. Ethylene glycol spray and heated induction air.
    - ☐ C. Alcohol spray and heated induction air.

18. The use of the carburetor air heater when it is not needed causes _____
    - ☐ A. a very lean mixture.
    - ☐ B. excessive increase in manifold pressure.
    - ☐ C. a decrease in power and possibly detonation.

19. Where would a carburetor air heater be located in a fuel injection system?
    - ☐ A. At the air intake entrance.
    - ☐ B. None is required.
    - ☐ C. Between the air intake and the venturi.

20. What directly regulates the speed of a turbo charger?
    - ☐ A. Turbine
    - ☐ B. Waste gate
    - ☐ C. Throttle

21. If the turbocharger waste gate is completely closed; _____
    - ☐ A. None of the exhaust gases are directed through the turbine.
    - ☐ B. The turbocharger is in the OFF position.
    - ☐ C. All the exhaust gases are directed through the turbine.

22. Boost manifold pressure is generally considered to be any manifold pressure above _____
    - ☐ A. 14.7 inches Hg.
    - ☐ B. 30 inches Hg.
    - ☐ C. 0 inches Hg.

23. The purpose of a bell mouth compressor inlet is to _____
    - ☐ A. provide an increased ram air effect at low air speeds.
    - ☐ B. maximize the aerodynamic efficiency of the inlet.
    - ☐ C. provide an increased pressure drop in the inlet.

24. If a fire starts in the induction system during the engine starting procedure, what should the operator do?
    - ☐ A. Turn off the fuel pump switches.
    - ☐ B. Continue cranking the engine.
    - ☐ C. Turn off the magneto switches.

25. On small aircraft engines, fuel vaporization may be increased by _____
    - ☐ A. cooling the air before it enters the engine.
    - ☐ B. circulating the fuel and air mixture through passages in the oil sump.
    - ☐ C. heating the fuel before it enters the carburetor.

Chapter 3, Final Chapter Exam - Induction and Exhaust Systems

Name:_____   Date:_____

PAGE LEFT BLANK INTENTIONALLY

IGNITION AND ELECTRICAL SYSTEMS

CHAPTER 4

Section A
Study Aid Questions - Fill In The Blanks

1. Ignition systems can be divided into two classifications: _____ systems or _____ systems for reciprocating engines.

2. _____ generally use one rotating magnet that feeds two complete magnetos in one magneto housing.

3. The _____ system is still the most widely used aircraft ignition system.

4. The magneto generates electrical power by the engine rotating the _____ and inducing a _____ flow in the coil windings.

5. Magneto operation is timed to the _____ so that a spark occurs only when the piston is on the _____ at a specified number of _____ before the top dead center _____ .

6. The high tension magneto system can be divided, for purposes of discussion, into 3 distinct circuits: _____ , _____ electrical, and _____ electrical circuits.

7. The magnetic circuit consists of a permanent multi-pole rotating _____ , a _____ , and _____ .

8. The _____ position produces the maximum number of _____ lines of force.

9. The _____ of the magnet is where one of the poles of the magnet is centered between the pole shoes of the magnetic circuit.

10. Most breaker points used in aircraft ignition systems are of the _____ type.

11. The secondary circuit contains the _____ of the _____ , _____ , _____ , _____ , and _____ .

12. When the primary circuit is _____ , the current flow through the primary coil produces _____ of force that cut across the secondary windings, inducing an _____ .

13. When the primary circuit current flow is _____ , the magnetic field surrounding the primary windings _____ .

14. Since most high-tension magnetos have many _____ of turns of wire in the _____ coil windings, a very _____ voltage is generated in the _____ .

15. _____ in any form is a good conductor of electricity.

IGNITION AND ELECTRICAL SYSTEMS

Section A
True of False

_____ 1. Flashover can lead to carbon tracking, which appears as a fine pencil like line on the unit across which flashover occurs.

_____ 2. The carbon trail results from the electric spark burning dirt particles that contain moisture.

_____ 3. Good magneto air circulation and ventilation also ensures that corrosive gases produced by normal arcing across the distributor air gap, such as ozone, are carried away.

_____ 4. A magneto is a high frequency radiation emanating (radio wave) device during its operation.

_____ 5. Capacitance is the ability to produce an electrostatic charge between two conducting plates connected by a dielectric.

_____ 6. In a pressurized magneto, the air is allowed to flow through and out of the magneto housing.

_____ 7. The ignition lead directs the electrical energy from the magneto to the spark plug.

_____ 8. Flange mounted magnetos are attached to the engine by a flange around the driven end of the rotating shaft of the magneto.

_____ 9. FADEC continuously monitors and controls only the fuel mixture/delivery/injection, as an integrated control system.

_____ 10. All opposed reciprocating engines are equipped with an impulse coupling as the auxiliary starting system.

Matching

Label the components on the following diagram.

1. _____   3. _____   5. _____

2. _____   4. _____

Match the number on the diagram with the correct term that describes the item.

_____ High Output Coil _____ Pinion Gear _____ Capacitor

_____ Distributor Block _____ Magnet _____ Ball Bearing

_____ Impulse Coupling _____ Cam _____ Distributor Gear

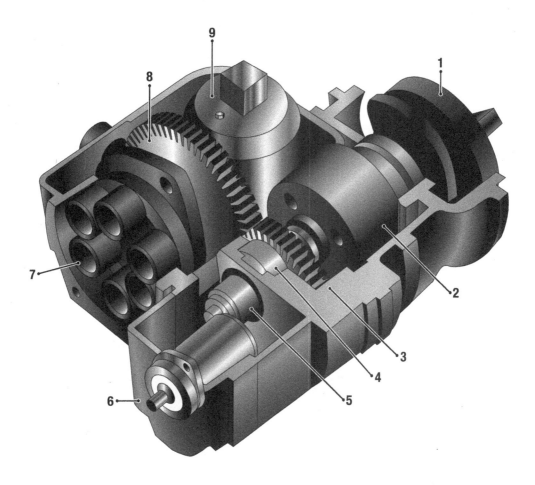

PAGE LEFT BLANK INTENTIONALLY

Section B
Knowledge Application Questions

1. What is the basic function of the starting vibrator and what kind of voltage does it produce?

2. Describe the function of the engines spark plug.

3. Describe the operating conditions that the spark plugs are subjected to during normal operation of the engine.

4. List the three main components of a spark plug.

   _____   _____   _____

5. What is the heat range of a spark plug?

6. What is spark plug reach?

7. What problems can occur if the ignition timing is too early?

8. What is meant by the top dead center piston position?

9. Describe the basic process of setting the e-gap of a basic magneto.

10. Describe a magneto check as part of an engine run-up check.

PAGE LEFT BLANK INTENTIONALLY

Section C
Final Chapter Exam

1. What is the purpose of a power check on a reciprocating engine?
    ☐ A. To check magneto drop.
    ☐ B. To determine satisfactory performance.
    ☐ C. To determine if the fuel/air mixture is adequate.

2. Dual magnetos generally use one rotating magnet that _____
    ☐ A. feeds two complete magnetos in one magneto housing.
    ☐ B. feeds a complete magneto in two magneto housings.
    ☐ C. feeds power to the generator.

3. The magneto, a special type of engine-driven Alternate Current (AC) generator, uses _____
    ☐ A. aircraft electrical system for power.
    ☐ B. a permanent magnet as a source of energy.
    ☐ C. a special generator that provides power to the magnetos.

4. The magneto generates electrical power by the engine rotating the _____
    ☐ A. permanent magnet and inducing a current to flow in the coil primary windings.
    ☐ B. engine driven generator.
    ☐ C. electrical system generator.

5. The primary electrical circuit consists of _____
    ☐ A. a permanent multi-pole rotating magnet, a soft iron core, and pole shoes.
    ☐ B. windings of the coil, distributor rotor, distributor cap, ignition lead, and spark plug.
    ☐ C. set of breaker contact points, a condenser, and an insulated coil.

6. The secondary circuit contains the _____
    ☐ A. a permanent multi-pole rotating magnet, a soft iron core, and pole shoes.
    ☐ B. windings of the coil, distributor rotor, distributor cap, ignition lead, and spark plug.
    ☐ C. set of breaker contact points, a condenser, and an insulated coil.

7. The magnetic circuit consists of _____
    ☐ A. a permanent multi-pole rotating magnet, a soft iron core, and pole shoes.
    ☐ B. windings of the coil, distributor rotor, distributor cap, ignition lead, and spark plug.
    ☐ C. set of breaker contact points, a condenser, and an insulated coil.

8. The component in the primary circuit, the condenser (capacitor), is wired _____
    ☐ A. in series with the breaker points.
    ☐ B. in parallel with the breaker points.
    ☐ C. is not wired to the breaker points.

9. Always take timing reading, or stop the propeller movement when setting up an engine for timing _____
    ☐ A. in the direction of rotation.
    ☐ B. opposite the direction of rotation.
    ☐ C. it makes no difference.

10. Inspection of ignition leads should include _____
    ☐ A. visual only.
    ☐ B. electrical only.
    ☐ C. a visual and an electrical test.

11. A spark plug is considered fouled _____
    ☐ A. if it has stopped allowing the spark to bridge the gap either completely of intermittently.
    ☐ B. if it is cover with oil.
    ☐ C. if it is covered with carbon.

IGNITION AND ELECTRICAL SYSTEMS

12. During the sparking of a spark plug the spark carries with it a portion of the electrode, part of which is _____
    - ☐ A. deposited on the other electrode.
    - ☐ B. some of the electrode is blown off in the combustion chamber.
    - ☐ C. both answers A and B.

13. The gap setting should be checked with _____
    - ☐ A. micrometer.
    - ☐ B. a round wire thickness gauge.
    - ☐ C. a flat-type thickness gauge.

14. The normal breaker contact surface has _____
    - ☐ A. a dull gray, sandblasted, almost rough appearance over the area where electrical contact is made.
    - ☐ B. well defined peaks extending noticeably above the surrounding surface.
    - ☐ C. deep pits in the surrounding surface.

15. The most common and difficult high-tension ignition system faults to detect are _____
    - ☐ A. high-voltage leaks.
    - ☐ B. low-voltage leaks.
    - ☐ C. magnetic problems.

16. The magnetic circuit of a magneto consists of a permanent multi-pole rotating magnet. The core is made of _____
    - ☐ A. hard steel.
    - ☐ B. soft iron.
    - ☐ C. electrical steel.

17. The E-gap angle is usually defined as the number of degrees between the neutral position of the rotating magnet and the position _____
    - ☐ A. where the contact points close.
    - ☐ B. where the contact points open.
    - ☐ C. the lowest magnetic flux density.

18. Why are high-tension ignition cables frequently routed from the distributors to the spark plugs in flexible metallic conduits?
    - ☐ A. To eliminate high altitude flashover.
    - ☐ B. To reduce the formation of corona and nitric oxide on the cable insulation.
    - ☐ C. To reduce the effect of high frequency electromagnetic waves emanated during operation.

19. What is the purpose of a safety gap in some magnetos?
    - ☐ A. To discharge the secondary coil's voltage if an open occurs in the secondary circuit.
    - ☐ B. To ground the magneto when the ignition switch is off.
    - ☐ C. To prevent flashover in the distributor.

20. When timing a magneto internally, the alignment of the timing marks indicates that the _____
    - ☐ A. breaker points are just closing.
    - ☐ B. magnets are in the neutral position.
    - ☐ C. magnets are in the E-gap position.

21. In a high-tension ignition system, the current in the magneto secondary winding is _____
    - ☐ A. conducted from the primary winding via the discharge of the capacitor.
    - ☐ B. induced when the primary circuit is interrupted.
    - ☐ C. induced when the primary circuit discharges via the breaker points.

22. Capacitance after-firing in most modern spark plugs is reduced by the use of _____
    - ☐ A. fine wire electrodes.
    - ☐ B. a built-in resistor in each plug.
    - ☐ C. aluminum oxide insulation.

23. As an aircraft engine's speed is increased, the voltage induced in the primary coil of the magneto _____
    ☐ A. remains constant.
    ☐ B. increases.
    ☐ C. varies with the setting of the voltage regulator.

24. The spark is produced in a magneto ignition system when the breaker points are _____
    ☐ A. fully open.
    ☐ B. beginning to open.
    ☐ C. fully closed.

25. What is the purpose of using an impulse coupling with a magneto?
    ☐ A. To absorb impulse vibrations between the magneto and the engine.
    ☐ B. To compensate for backlash in the magneto and the engine gears.
    ☐ C. To produce a momentary high rotational speed of the magneto.

Chapter 4, Final Chapter Exam - Ignition and Electrical Systems

Name:_____ Date:_____

PAGE LEFT BLANK INTENTIONALLY

STARTING SYSTEMS

Section A
Study Aid Questions - Fill In The Blanks

1. Both reciprocating and turbine aircraft engines require help during the _____ .

2. _____ engine starters have a critical role to play in the starting of the engine.

3. _____ starters are driven by compressed air through a _____ that is mechanically connected through reduction gears to one of the engine's _____ .

4. Almost all _____ use a form of electric motor geared to the engine.

5. Modern _____ use electric motors, starter/generators (electric motor and a generator in the same housing) and _____ starters.

6. All starting systems have operating _____ because of the _____ uses during cranking or rotation of the engine.

7. The type of starter that has starter limits uses the limit of, after energizing the starter for _____ , it should be allowed to cool for at least _____ After a second or subsequent cranking period of _____ , it should cool for _____ .

8. A _____ is activated by either a push button or turning the ignition key on the instrument panel.

9. Gas turbine engines are started by rotating the _____ .

10. To start a _____ engine it is necessary to accelerate the compressor to provide sufficient _____ to support combustion.

11. The starter must continue to assist the engine to a speed above the _____ .

12. As soon as the starter has accelerated the compressor sufficiently to establish airflow through the engine, the _____ is turned on, and then the _____ .

13. If assistance from the starter were cut off below the _____ , the engine would most likely fail to accelerate to idle speed.

14. The typical air turbine starter consists of an _____ which turns a drive coupling through a _____ train and a _____ .

15. The air turbine starter is operated by introducing air of sufficient _____ and _____ into the starter inlet.

STARTING SYSTEMS

Section A
True of False

_____ 1. Once the reciprocating engine has fired and has started, the starter is engaged.

_____ 2. Reciprocating engines need only to be turned through at a relatively slow speed until the engine starts and turns on its own.

_____ 3. In the early stages of aircraft development, relatively low-powered reciprocating engines were started by pulling the propeller through a part of a revolution by hand.

_____ 4. In a typical low-horsepower reciprocating engine starting system, the direct-cranking turbine starter consists of two basic components: a motor assembly and a gear section.

_____ 5. Most starting system maintenance practices include replacing the starter motor brushes and brush springs, cleaning dirty commutators, and turning down burned or out-of-round starter commutators.

_____ 6. As a rule, starter brushes should be replaced when worn down to approximately one-half their original length.

_____ 7. Emery paper or carborundum should be used for cleaning the commutator because of their possible shorting action.

_____ 8. Roughness, out-of-roundness, or high-mica conditions are all reasons for not turning down the commutator.

_____ 9. During starter maintenance the drive gear should be checked for wear along with the ring gear.

_____ 10. On some turbine engine installations, at the proper points in the sequence, during the starting of a turbine engine, the starter and ignition will be automatically cut off.

Section A
Matching

Place the letter of the probable causes in the blank that is the correct trouble.

_____External oil leakage.

_____Broken nozzle vanes.

_____Starter will not cut off.

_____Oil leakage at drive coupling.

_____Starter inlet will not line up with
supply ducting.

_____Starter does not operate (no rotation).

_____Oil leakage from vent plug assembly.

_____Starter runs but engine won't turn over.

_____Starter will not accelerate to normal
cutoff speed.

_____Metallic particles on magnetic drain plug.

Air Turbine Starter System Troubleshooting Procedures	
Probable Cause	**Remedy**
(A) · No air supply · Electrical open in cutout switch · Sheared starter drive coupling · Internal starter discrepancy	· Check air supply. · Check switch continuity. If no continuity, remove starter and adjust or replace switch. · Remove starter and replace drive coupling. · Remove and replace starter.
(B) · Low starter air supply · Starter cutout switch set improperly · Valve pressure regulated too low · Internal starter malfunction	· Check air source pressure. · Adjust rotor switch actuator. · Replace valve. · Remove and replace starter.
(C) · Low air supply · Rotor switch actuator set too high · Starter cutout switch shorted	· Check air supply. · Adjust switch actuator assembly. · Replace switch and bracket assembly.
(D) · Oil level too high · Loose vent, oil filler, or magnetic plugs · Loose clamp band assembly	· Drain oil and re-service properly. · Tighten magnetic plug to proper torque. · Tighten vent and oil filler plugs as necessary and lock wire. Tighten clamp band assembly to higher torque.
(E) · Sheared drive coupling	· Remove starter and replace the drive coupling. If couplings persist in breaking in unusually short periods of time, remove and replace starter.
(F) · Improper installation of starter on engine, or improper indexing of turbine housing on starter	· Check installation and/or indexing for conformance with manufacturer's installation instructions and the proper index position of the turbine housing specified for the aircraft.
(G) · Small fuzzy particles indicate normal wear · Particles coarser than fuzzy (chips, slivers, etc.) indicate internal difficulty	· No remedial action required. · Remove and replace starter.
(H) · Large foreign particles in air supply	· Remove and replace starter and check air supply filter.
(I) · Improper starter installation position	· Check installed position for levelness of oil plugs and correct as required in accordance with manufacturer's installation instructions.
(J) · Leaking rear seal assembly	· Remove and replace starter.

PAGE LEFT BLANK INTENTIONALLY

Section B
Knowledge Application Questions

1. What is the role and importance of the starter in starting a turbine engine?

2. Describe the typical starter voltage, windings, and type of torque developed by reciprocating starters.

3. In a typical high-horsepower reciprocating engine starting system, what two basic components make up the starting system?

4. What is the sequence of events that take place as the start cycle is activated?

5. Explain the operational sequence of a starting system which uses an electric starter motor and a ring gear on a propeller hub.

6. Describe the procedure for cleaning or reconditioning a starter with a glazed or dirty commutator.

7. When starting a turbine engine, what would happen if the starter was cut off below a self-sustaining speed?

8. What are the sources of air to operate an air turbine starter?

9. Describe the operation of the air turbine starter.

10. What is the air source for operating air turbine starters?

Chapter 5, Section B - Starting Systems

Name:_____   Date:_____

PAGE LEFT BLANK INTENTIONALLY

Section C
Final Chapter Exam

1. Once the reciprocating engine has fired and has started, the starter is _____
   ☐ A. disengaged.
   ☐ B. engaged.
   ☐ C. turned on.

2. In the case of a turbine engine the starter must turn the engine _____
   ☐ A. always clockwise to provide enough air flow through the engine.
   ☐ B. always counter clockwise to provide enough air flow through the engine.
   ☐ C. up to a speed to provide enough air flow through the engine.

3. The most widely used starting system on all types of reciprocating engines utilizes _____
   ☐ A. the direct-cranking electric starter.
   ☐ B. the in-direct-cranking electric starter.
   ☐ C. hand inertia starters.

4. Gas turbine engines are started by rotating the _____
   ☐ A. low pressure spool.
   ☐ B. high pressure compressor.
   ☐ C. turbine wheel.

5. The air turbine starters are designed to provide _____
   ☐ A. high starting torque.
   ☐ B. low starting torque.
   ☐ C. high starting speed.

6. As a rule, starter brushes should be replaced when worn down to approximately _____
   ☐ A. one-third the original length.
   ☐ B. one-half the original length.
   ☐ C. two-third the original length.

7. A glazed or dirty starter commutator can be cleaned by holding a _____
   ☐ A. carborundum against the commutator as it is turned.
   ☐ B. emery paper against the commutator as it is turned.
   ☐ C. strip of double-00 sandpaper or a brush seating stone against the commutator as it is turned.

8. While acting as a starter, the starter generator can use up to _____
   ☐ A. 1,500 peak amps.
   ☐ B. 1,000 peak amps.
   ☐ C. 500 peak amps.

9. The typical air turbine starter weighs _____
   ☐ A. one-fourth to one-half as much as an electric starter capable of starting the same engine.
   ☐ B. three-fourths as much as an electric starter capable of starting the same engine.
   ☐ C. about the same as much as an electric starter capable of starting the same engine.

10. To activate an air turbine starter _____
    ☐ A. the bleed valve and the start valve must be open.
    ☐ B. the bleed valve and the start valve must be closed.
    ☐ C. the bleed valve open and the start valve closed.

11. When using an electric starter motor, the current flow through it _____
    ☐ A. is highest just before starter cutoff (at highest RPM).
    ☐ B. remains relatively constant throughout the starting cycle.
    ☐ C. is highest at the start of motor rotation.

STARTING SYSTEMS

12. While performing maintenance on helicopters, technicians usually include checking the _____
    - ☐ A. oil level and magnetic drain plug condition.
    - ☐ B. stator and rotor blades for FOD.
    - ☐ C. rotor alignment.

13. Airflow to the pneumatic starter from a ground unit is normally prevented from causing starter overspeed during engine start by _____
    - ☐ A. stator nozzle design that chokes airflow and stabilizes turbine wheel speed.
    - ☐ B. activation of a flyweight cutout switch.
    - ☐ C. a preset timed cutoff of the airflow at the source.

14. The purpose of an undercurrent relay in a starter generator system is to _____
    - ☐ A. provide a backup for the starter relay.
    - ☐ B. disconnect power from the starter-generator and ignition when sufficient engine speed is reached.
    - ☐ C. keep current flow to the starter-generator under the circuit capacity maximum.

15. In a typical starter-generator system, under which of the following starting circumstances may it be necessary to use the start stop switch?
    - ☐ A. Normal lite off start.
    - ☐ B. Hot start.
    - ☐ C. Contacts stick open.

16. In an inertia starter, energy is started slowly during an energizing process by a _____
    - ☐ A. direct cranking starter.
    - ☐ B. manual hand crank.
    - ☐ C. starter mote.

17. What is a starter ring mounted to?
    - ☐ A. Propeller flyweights.
    - ☐ B. Starter motor.
    - ☐ C. Propeller hub.

18. If an electrical starter drags the probable cause could be _____
    - ☐ A. master switch.
    - ☐ B. low battery.
    - ☐ C. starter switch.

19. A starter generator is permanently engaged _____
    - ☐ A. with the engine shaft drive gears.
    - ☐ B. with an air supply.
    - ☐ C. bleed air from the compressor.

20. The typical air turbine starter consist _____
    - ☐ A. an axial flow turbine.
    - ☐ B. centrifugal turbine.
    - ☐ C. no turbine is used.

21. Air turbine starters can be supplied with pressure air from _____
    - ☐ A. ground cart supply.
    - ☐ B. external gearbox.
    - ☐ C. air control valve.

22. When the start air control valve is open on an air turbine start system the engine is _____
    - ☐ A. this valve will not cause the engine to turn until the ignition is on.
    - ☐ B. the engine is not turning.
    - ☐ C. the engine is turning.

23. An air turbine starter system fails to rotate the cause could be _____
    □ A. external oil leakage.
    □ B. no air supply.
    □ C. leaking rear seal assembly.

24. In a typical direct cranking electrical starter system what component closes to provide power to the starter?
    □ A. Master switch.
    □ B. Starter switch.
    □ C. Starter solenoid.

25. How is the cartridge ignited in a cartridge-pneumatic turbine engine starter system?
    □ A. Hot gas nozzles.
    □ B. Relief valves.
    □ C. By applying voltage through the breech handle.

Chapter 5, Final Chapter Exam - Starting Systems

Name:_____ Date:_____

PAGE LEFT BLANK INTENTIONALLY

ENGINE LUBRICATION

CHAPTER 6

1. The primary purpose of a lubricant is to reduce _____ between _____ parts.

2. _____ is generally pumped throughout the engine to all areas that require _____ .

3. Overcoming the _____ of the moving parts of the engine consumes _____ and creates unwanted _____ .

4. _____ is when one surface slides over another surface such as in _____ bearings.

5. _____ is when a roller or sphere rolls over another surface such as with _____ or _____ bearings also referred to as _____ bearings.

6. _____ which occurs between gear teeth is a type of friction in which pressure can vary widely and the _____ applied to the gears can be _____ .

7. Oil _____ can account for up to _____% of the total engine _____ and is a great medium to transfer the _____ from the engine to the oil _____ .

8. The oil film acts as a _____ between metal parts.

9. Oil _____ the engine by reducing abrasive wear by picking up foreign particles and carrying them to a _____ .

10. Oil prevents _____ on the interior of the engine by leaving a _____ of oil on parts when the engine is shut down. This coating of oil prevents _____ but will not last on the parts allowing them to eventually _____ or _____ .

11. The oil selected for engine lubrication must be light enough to circulate freely at _____ , yet heavy enough to provide the proper oil film at engine _____ .

12. The _____ is a number that indicates the effect of temperature changes on the _____ of the oil.

13. Oil tanks are generally associated with a _____ system.

14. The oil filter _____ , located between the pressure side of the oil pump the oil filter, permits unfiltered oil to bypass the filter and enter the engine if the oil filter is _____ .

15. _____ allows an oil sample to be analyzed and searched for the presence of minute metallic elements.

ENGINE LUBRICATION

Section A
True of False

_____ 1. The advantages of oil analysis are increases in safety by noticing an engine problem before engine failure.

_____ 2. The exhaust turbine bearing is the most critical lubricating point in a gas turbine engine because of the high temperature normally present.

_____ 3. In some turbine engines air cooling is used instead of oil cooling for the bearing which supports the turbine.

_____ 4. Only dry-sump lubrication systems are used in gas turbine engines.

_____ 5. All oil tanks are provided with expansion space.

_____ 6. The scavenge elements have a lesser pumping capacity than the pressure element to prevent oil from collecting in the bearing sumps of the engine.

_____ 7. A regulating (relief) valve in the discharge side of the pump limits the output pressure of the pump by passing oil to the pump inlet when the outlet pressure exceeds a predetermined limit.

_____ 8. Oil normally flows through the filter element from the outside into the filter body.

_____ 9. If the last-chance filters in the oil jets should become clogged, bearing failure usually will not be the result, since nozzles are easily accessible for cleaning.

_____ 10. The oil pressure differential oil pressure switch (light or indicator) alerts the flight crew of an impending oil filter bypass because of a clogged filter.

Section A
Matching

The examples below show some metals and suggested areas of the engine that could be the source of the wear metals. Match the metal with the possible wearing or failing engine components.

A. Iron	C. Aluminum	E. Tin	G. Titanium	I. Phosphorous
B. Chromium	D. Nickel	F. Silver	H. Molybdenum	J. Lead

1. _____ Wear originating from rings, shafts, gears, valve train, cylinder walls, and pistons.

2. _____ Primary sources are chromed parts such as rings, liners, etc., and some coolant additives.

3. _____ Indicates wear of pistons, rod bearings and certain types of bushings.

4. _____ Secondary indicator of wear from certain types of bearings, shafts, valves and valve guides.

5. _____ Indicates wear from bearings.

6. _____ Wear of bearings which contain silver. In some instances, a secondary indicator of oil cooler problems.

7. _____ Alloy in high quality steel for gears and bearings.

8. _____ Indicates gear or ring wear. Used as an additive in some oils.

9. _____ Antirust agents, spark-plug and combustion chamber deposits.

10. _____ Mostly from tetraethyl lead contamination.

Section B
Knowledge Application Questions

1. Discuss the functions of engine oil.

2. Why does the oil used in aircraft reciprocating engines have a relatively high viscosity?

3. What is Viscosity Index?

4. What are the advantages of pressure lubrication?

5. What is the function of the oil pressure regulating valve?

6. Explain how the oil pump pressurizes the oil as it passes through it.

7. What are the main types of contaminants that oil, in service, is constantly exposed.

8. Explain the procedure for inspecting the pressure oil filter element and the suction screen.

9. Where are oil jets or nozzles located? What type of bearings do they lubricate? Explain their operation.

10. Explain the operation of the exhaust gas temperature indicator system for reciprocating engines.

PAGE LEFT BLANK INTENTIONALLY

Section C
Final Chapter Exam

1. Engine oil temperature gauges indicate the temperature of the oil _____
   ☐ A. entering the oil cooler.
   ☐ B. entering the engine.
   ☐ C. in the oil storage tank.

2. What prevents pressure within the lubricating oil tank from rising above or falling below ambient pressure (reciprocating engine)?
   ☐ A. Oil tank check valve.
   ☐ B. Oil pressure relief valve.
   ☐ C. Oil tank vent.

3. In a jet engine which uses a fuel oil heat exchanger, the oil temperature is controlled by a thermostatic valve that regulates the flow of _____
   ☐ A. fuel through the heat exchanger.
   ☐ B. both fuel and oil through the heat exchanger.
   ☐ C. oil through the heat exchanger.

4. What is the purpose of the last chance oil filters?
   ☐ A. To prevent damage to the oil spray nozzle.
   ☐ B. To filter the oil immediately before it enters the main bearings.
   ☐ C. To assure a clean supply of oil to the lubrication system.

5. Which of the following is a function of the fuel oil heat exchanger on a turbine engine?
   ☐ A. Aerates the fuel.
   ☐ B. Emulsifies the oil.
   ☐ C. Increases fuel temperature.

6. In a reciprocating engine oil system, the temperature bulb senses oil temperature _____
   ☐ A. at a point after the oil has passed through the oil cooler.
   ☐ B. while the oil is in the hottest area of the engine.
   ☐ C. immediately before the oil enters the oil cooler.

7. Why are fixed orifice nozzles used in the lubrication system of gas turbine engines?
   ☐ A. To provide a relatively constant oil flow to the main bearings at all engine speeds.
   ☐ B. To keep back pressure on the oil pump, thus preventing an air lock.
   ☐ C. To protect the oil seals by preventing excessive pressure from entering the bearing cavities.

8. At cruise RPM, some oil will flow through the relief valve of a gear type engine oil pump. This is normal as the relief valve is set at a pressure which is _____
   ☐ A. lower than the pump inlet pressure.
   ☐ B. lower than the pressure pump capabilities.
   ☐ C. higher than pressure pump capabilities.

9. What will happen to the return oil if the oil line between the scavenger pump and the oil cooler separates?
   ☐ A. Oil will accumulate in the engine.
   ☐ B. The return oil will be pumped overboard.
   ☐ C. The scavenger return line check valve will close and force the oil to bypass directly to the intake side of the pressure pump.

10. The oil dampened main bearing utilized in some turbine engines is used to _____
    ☐ A. provide lubrication of bearings from the beginning of starting rotation until normal oil pressure is established.
    ☐ B. provide an oil film between the outer race and the bearing housing in order to reduce vibration tendencies in the rotor system, and to allow for slight misalignment.
    ☐ C. dampen surges in oil pressure to the bearings.

ENGINE LUBRICATION

11. The engine oil temperature regulator is usually located between which of the following on a dry sump reciprocating engine?
    ☐ A. The engine oil supply pump and the internal lubrication system.
    ☐ B. The scavenger pump outlet and the oil storage tank.
    ☐ C. The oil storage tank and the engine oil supply pump.

12. After making a welded repair to a pressurized turbine engine oil tank, the tank should be pressure checked to _____
    ☐ A. not less than 5 psi plus the maximum operating pressure of the tank.
    ☐ B. not less than 5 psi plus the average operating pressure of the tank.
    ☐ C. 5 psi.

13. Possible failure related ferrous metal particles in turbine engine oil cause an (electrical) indicating type magnetic chip detector to indicate their presence by _____
    ☐ A. disturbing the magnetic lines of flux around the detector tip.
    ☐ B. bridging the gap between the detector center (positive) electrode and the ground electrode.
    ☐ C. generating a small electric current that is caused by the particles being in contact with the dissimilar metal of the detector tip.

14. What would be the probable result if the oil system pressure relief valve should stick in the open position on a turbine engine?
    ☐ A. Increased oil pressure.
    ☐ B. Decreased oil temperature.
    ☐ C. Insufficient lubrication.

15. What is the primary purpose of the oil to fuel heat exchanger?
    ☐ A. Cool the fuel.
    ☐ B. Cool the oil.
    ☐ C. De-aerate the oil.

16. Low oil pressure can be detrimental to the internal engine components. However, high oil pressure _____
    ☐ A. should be limited to the engine manufacturer's recommendations.
    ☐ B. has a negligible effect.
    ☐ C. will not occur because of pressure losses around the bearings.

17. What is the primary purpose of the oil breather pressurization system that is used on turbine engines?
    ☐ A. Prevents foaming of the oil and keeps internal pressures equal.
    ☐ B. Allows aeration of the oil for better lubrication because of the air/oil mist.
    ☐ C. Provides a proper oil spray pattern from the main bearing oil jets.

18. What is the source of most of the heat that is absorbed by the lubricating oil in a reciprocating engine?
    ☐ A. Crankshaft main bearings.
    ☐ B. Exhaust valves.
    ☐ C. Pistons and cylinder walls.

19. What type of oil system is usually found on turbine engines?
    ☐ A. Dry sump, pressure, and spray.
    ☐ B. Dry sump, dip, and splash.
    ☐ C. Wet sump, spray, and splash.

20. What will be the result of operating an engine in extremely high temperatures using a lubricant recommended by the manufacturer for a much lower temperature?
    ☐ A. The oil pressure will be higher than normal.
    ☐ B. The oil temperature and oil pressure will be higher than normal.
    ☐ C. The oil pressure will be lower than normal.

21. Regarding the below statements:
    01. Gas turbine and reciprocating engine oils can be mixed or used interchangeably.
    02. Most gas turbine engine oils are synthetic.
    ☐ A. Only No. 02 is true.
    ☐ B. Both No. 01 and No. 02 are true.
    ☐ C. Neither No. 01 or No. 02 is true.

22. The time in seconds required for exactly 60 cubic centimeters of oil to flow through an accurately calibrated orifice at a specific temperature is recorded as a measurement of the oil's _____
    ☐ A. flash point.
    ☐ B. specific gravity.
    ☐ C. viscosity.

23. Upon what quality or characteristic of a lubricating oil is its viscosity index based?
    ☐ A. Its resistance to flow at a standard temperature as compared to high grade paraffin base oil at the same temperature.
    ☐ B. Its rate of change in viscosity with temperature change
    ☐ C. Its rate of flow through an orifice at a standard temperature

24. Compared to reciprocating engine oils, the types of oils used in turbine engines _____
    ☐ A. are required to carry and disperse a higher level of combustion byproducts.
    ☐ B. may permit a somewhat higher level of carbon formation in the engine.
    ☐ C. have less tendency to produce lacquer or coke.

25. The oil used in reciprocating engines has a relatively high viscosity due to _____
    ☐ A. the reduced ability of thin oils to maintain adequate film strength at altitude (reduced atmospheric pressure).
    ☐ B. the relatively high rotational speeds.
    ☐ C. large clearances and high operating temperatures.

Chapter 6, Final Chapter Exam - Engine Lubrication

Name:_____   Date:_____

PAGE LEFT BLANK INTENTIONALLY

PROPELLERS

Section A
Study Aid Questions - Fill In The Blanks

1. All propeller driven aircraft are limited by the _____ at which propellers can be turned.

2. The power needed to rotate the propeller blades is furnished by the _____ .

3. _____ is the difference between the _____ pitch of the propeller and its _____ pitch.

4. _____ pitch is the distance a propeller should advance in one revolution with no slippage.

5. _____ pitch is the distance it actually advances.

6. _____ is a physical force that tends to throw the rotating propeller blades away from the hub.

7. _____ force in the form of air resistance, tends to bend the propeller blades opposite to the direction of rotation.

8. _____ force is the thrust load that tends to bend propeller blades forward as the aircraft is pulled through the air.

9. _____ force tends to turn the blades to a high blade angle.

10. _____ force, being greater than the aerodynamic twisting force, tries to force the blades toward a low blade angle.

11. _____ propellers have no controls and require no adjustments in flight.

12. The _____ propeller has a propeller control in the center pedestal between the _____ and the _____ control and is colored _____ .

13. A _____ is used to test and break-in reciprocating engines.

14. Constant speed propellers have an opposing force that operates against the _____ from the governor.

15. When the engine is operating below the RPM set by the pilot using the cockpit control, the governor is operating in an _____ .

16. When the engine is operating above the RPM set by the pilot using the cockpit control, the governor is operating in an _____ .

17. When the engine is operating at the RPM set by the pilot using the cockpit control, the governor is operating _____ .

18. A _____ propeller is a constant speed propeller used on multiengine aircraft having a mechanism to change the pitch to an angle to around 90°.

19. The purpose of the _____ is to produce a negative blade angle which will produce thrust opposite the normal forward direction.

20. An _____ control system consists basically of an electrical energy source, a resistance heating element, system controls, and necessary wiring.

Section A
True of False

_____ 1. The propeller is the unit which must absorb the power output of the engine.

_____ 2. There are several forces acting on the propeller as it turns, one of the major forces is centrifugal force.

_____ 3. The aircraft speed of a propeller driven aircraft is limited to around 600 MPH.

_____ 4. An airplane moving through the air creates a lifting force opposing its forward motion.

_____ 5. The work done by the thrust is equal to the thrust times the distance it moves the airplane (Work = Thrust × Distance).

_____ 6. The engine supplies brake horsepower through a rotating shaft, and the propeller converts it into indicated horsepower.

_____ 7. Geometric pitch is usually expressed in pitch inches.

_____ 8. The shape of the propeller blade creates thrust, because it is like the shape of a wing.

_____ 9. Fixed-pitch and ground-adjustable propellers are designed for best efficiency at one rotation and forward speed.

_____ 10. During takeoff, when maximum power and thrust are required, the constant-speed propeller is at a high propeller blade angle or pitch.

Matching

Identify each component in the drawing by the terms below:

Pilot controls   Speeder Spring   1. _____   3. _____

Flyweights   Pilot Valve   2. _____   4. _____

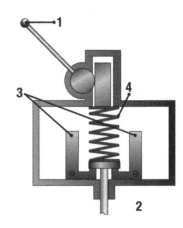

Identify each component in the pitch change mechanism drawing below:

1. Blade Actuating Lever   4. Servo Piston Dome
2. Oil Transfer Sleeve   5. Feathering Spring
3. Propeller Governor   6. Spider Hub

1. _____   4. _____

2. _____   5. _____

3. _____   6. _____

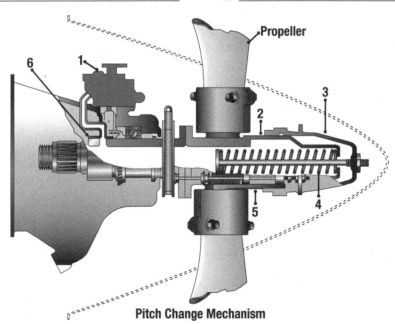

Pitch Change Mechanism

Chapter 7, Section A - Propellers

Name:_____   Date:_____

PAGE LEFT BLANK INTENTIONALLY

Section B
Knowledge Application Questions

1. Describe thrust horsepower.

2. Where the stress is greatest on propellers, what type of force is it and what increases this stress?

3. Describe a tractor type propeller.

4. What is a controllable-pitch propeller?

5. Explain propeller governor operation.

6. Describe a propeller synchronization system.

7. Explain the operation of an auto-feather system.

8. List the procedure for inspecting composite blades.

9. Describe the procedure for tracking propeller blades.

10. What are the advantages of dynamic propeller balancing?

PAGE LEFT BLANK INTENTIONALLY

Section C
Final Chapter Exam

1. A Cessna 180 aircraft has a McCauley propeller Model No. 2A34C50/90A. The propeller is severely damaged in a ground accident, and this model propeller is not available for replacement. Which of the following should be used to find an approved alternate replacement?
   ☐ A. Summary of Supplemental Type Certificates.
   ☐ B. Aircraft Specifications/Type Certificate Data Sheets.
   ☐ C. Aircraft Engine and Propeller Specifications/Type Certificate Data Sheets.

2. Aluminum propeller blade failure at the site of an unrepaired nick or scratch is usually the result of _____
   ☐ A. material defect.
   ☐ B. intergranular corrosion.
   ☐ C. stress concentration.

3. Propeller blade stations are measured from the _____
   ☐ A. hub centerline.
   ☐ B. blade butt.
   ☐ C. blade centerline.

4. The actual distance a propeller moves forward through the air during one revolution is known as the _____
   ☐ A. geometric pitch.
   ☐ B. effective pitch.
   ☐ C. relative pitch.

5. The centrifugal twisting moment of an operating propeller tends to _____
   ☐ A. increase pitch angle.
   ☐ B. reduce pitch angle.
   ☐ C. bend the blades in the direction of rotation.

6. Which of the following functions requires the use of a propeller blade station?
   ☐ A. Propeller balancing.
   ☐ B. Indexing blades.
   ☐ C. Measuring blade angle.

7. Counterweights on constant-speed propellers are generally used to aid in _____
   ☐ A. increase blade angle.
   ☐ B. un-feathering the propeller.
   ☐ C. decreasing blade angle.

8. The blade angle of a fixed pitch propeller _____
   ☐ A. is greatest at the tip.
   ☐ B. is smallest at the tip.
   ☐ C. increases in proportion to the distance each section is from the hub.

9. What operational force tends to increase propeller blade angle?
   ☐ A. Centrifugal twisting force.
   ☐ B. Aerodynamic twisting force.
   ☐ C. Thrust bending force.

10. What unit in the propeller anti-icing system controls the output of the pump?
    ☐ A. Pressure relief valve.
    ☐ B. Rheostat.
    ☐ C. Cycling timer.

PROPELLERS

11. How is aircraft electrical power for propeller deicer systems transferred from the engine to the propeller hub assembly?
    - ☐ A. By slip rings and segment plates.
    - ☐ B. By flexible electrical connectors.
    - ☐ C. By slip ring and brushes.

12. What actuates the pilot valve in the governor of a constant speed propeller?
    - ☐ A. Engine oil pressure.
    - ☐ B. Governor flyweights.
    - ☐ C. Governor pump oil pressure.

13. The primary reason for careful inspection and prompt repairing of minor surface defects such as scratches, nicks, gouges, on aluminum alloy propellers is to prevent _____
    - ☐ A. corrosion.
    - ☐ B. unbalanced aerodynamics.
    - ☐ C. fatigue failure.

14. What operational force tends to bend the propeller blades forward at the tips?
    - ☐ A. Torque bending force.
    - ☐ B. Centrifugal twisting force.
    - ☐ C. Thrust bending force.

15. The primary purpose of a propeller is to _____
    - ☐ A. create lift on the fixed airfoils of an aircraft.
    - ☐ B. change engine horsepower to thrust.
    - ☐ C. provide static and dynamic stability of an aircraft in flight.

16. How is anti-icing fluid ejected from the slinger ring on a propeller?
    - ☐ A. By pump pressure.
    - ☐ B. By centripetal force.
    - ☐ C. By centrifugal force.

17. Propeller fluid anti-icing systems generally use which of the following?
    - ☐ A. Ethylene glycol.
    - ☐ B. Isopropyl alcohol.
    - ☐ C. Ethyl alcohol.

18. Ice formation on a propeller blade will _____
    - ☐ A. produce unbalance and vibration.
    - ☐ B. increase thrust and drag.
    - ☐ C. cause a change in blade angle.

19. Which of the following is used to correct horizontal unbalance of a wood propeller?
    - ☐ A. Brass screws.
    - ☐ B. Shellac.
    - ☐ C. Solder.

20. When engine power is increased, the constant-speed propeller tries to function so that it will _____
    - ☐ A. maintain the RPM, decrease the blade angle, and maintain a low angle of attack.
    - ☐ B. increase the RPM, decrease the blade angle, and maintain a low angle of attack.
    - ☐ C. maintain the RPM, increase the blade angle, and maintain a low angle of attack.

21. The propeller governor controls the _____
    - ☐ A. oil to and from the pitch changing mechanism.
    - ☐ B. spring tension on the boost pump speeder spring.
    - ☐ C. linkage and counterweights from moving in and out.

22. What actuates the pilot valve in the governor of a constant-speed propeller?
    ☐ A. Engine oil pressure.
    ☐ B. Governor flyweights.
    ☐ C. Governor pump oil pressure.

23. When the centrifugal force acting on the propeller governor flyweights overcomes the tension on the speeder spring, a propeller is in what speed condition?
    ☐ A. On speed.
    ☐ B. Underspeed.
    ☐ C. Overspeed.

24. What operational force tends to increase propeller blade angle?
    ☐ A. Centrifugal twisting force.
    ☐ B. Aerodynamic twisting force.
    ☐ C. Thrust bending force.

25. The actual distance a propeller moves forward through the air during one revolution is known as the
    _____
    ☐ A. effective pitch.
    ☐ B. geometric pitch.
    ☐ C. relative pitch.

Chapter 7, Final Chapter Exam - Propellers

Name:_____ Date:_____

PROPELLERS

PAGE LEFT BLANK INTENTIONALLY

Section A
Study Aid Questions - Fill In The Blanks

1. Engine life is dependent upon such factors as _____, the quality of _____ or overhaul, the type of aircraft in which the engine is installed, the kind of _____ being carried out, and the degree which _____ is accomplished.

2. The _____ will set engine removal times based on _____ experience.

3. Sudden stoppage is a very rapid and complete _____ of the engine.

4. Sudden stoppage can be caused by _____ or by one or more of the _____ striking an object in such a way that RPM goes to zero in less than _____ complete revolution of the propeller.

5. _____ in the engine oil screens or the magnetic chip detectors are generally an indication of partial internal _____ of the engine.

6. Before removing an engine for suspected internal failure as indicated by foreign material on the oil screens or oil sump plugs, determine if the foreign particles are _____ metal by placing them close to see if they are _____ .

7. Any _____ metal in the oil screens is cause for _____ .

8. _____ allows an oil sample to be analyzed and searched for the presence of minute metallic elements.

9. Oil analysis programs identify and measures particles in _____ by weight.

10. Many turbine engines are monitored by an _____ which helps determine the health of the engine in service.

11. Before installing any replacement accessory, check it visually for signs of _____ and for _____ .

12. The _____ is a framework, covered with 'removable cowling, in which the engine is mounted. This assembly is attached to the aircraft and incorporates an insulating firewall between the engine and the airframe.

ENGINE REMOVAL AND REPLACEMENT

13. The engine mounting _____ are usually checked for condition by magnetic particle inspection or other approved process.

14. Inspect the exhaust stacks, collector ring, and tailpipe assembly for _____ , or _____ , or _____ .

15. Before the new engine is flight-tested, it must undergo a thorough _____ .

Section A
True of False

_____ 1. To prevent failure of the engine bearings during the initial start, the engine should be pre-oiled.

_____ 2. When no external means of pre-oiling an engine are available, the engine oil pump may be used.

_____ 3. Generally, the engine should be operated within 30 minutes after it has been pre-oiled; otherwise, the pre-oiling procedure normally must be repeated.

_____ 4. The manufacturer's instructions should always be used as a guide in engine removal or installation.

_____ 5. On turbine engine aircraft, the power levers must be rigged so that they are aligned at all power settings.

_____ 6. Most computer controlled engines have an electronic connection from the flight deck to the push pull control rods and cables.

_____ 7. The fuel control unit of the engine is adjusted to trim the engine in order that the minimum thrust output of the engine can be obtained when desired.

_____ 8. The engine must be re-trimmed when a fuel control unit is replaced, when the engine does not develop maximum thrust, engine change or excessive throttle stagger.

_____ 9. If wind velocity is a factor, the aircraft should be headed into the wind while trimming or checking the trim on an engine.

_____ 10. An engine should never be trimmed when icing conditions exist because of the adverse effects on trimming accuracy.

Matching

Using the diagram to the right match the numbered items on the diagram to the correct items listed.

_____ Upper Shroud

_____ Bleed Air Flange

_____ Fuel Heater

_____ Cradle Base

_____ Lock Handle

_____ Bleed Air Valve

_____ EGT Receptacle

_____ Bleed Air Duct Coupling

_____ Engine Mount Bracket

_____ Fire Extinguisher Line Fitting

_____ EGT Plug

_____ Compressor Plenum

_____ Bonding Jumper

_____ Hoist Assembly

_____ Bleed Air Duct

_____ Engine Mount Bracket and Vibration Isolator

_____ Fire Detection Sensor Element Receptacle

_____ Electrical Plug for the Generator Control

_____ Receptacle for APU Electrical Generator

_____ Electrical Plug for the Starter Motor

_____ Accessory Cooling Air Duct Flange

_____ Receptacle for Generator Control

_____ Receptacle for Starter Motor

_____ Electrical Plug for the APU Harness

_____ Receptacle for the APU Harness

_____ Bleed Load Control Air Line Fitting

_____ Electrical Plug for the APU Generator

Chapter 8, Section A - Engine Removal and Replacement

Name:_____ Date:_____

ENGINE REMOVAL AND REPLACEMENT

PAGE LEFT BLANK INTENTIONALLY

Section B
Knowledge Application Questions

1. What determines engine life or length of engine service?

2. Define engine sudden stoppage.

3. Why should material in the oil screen or oil sump plugs be tested before removing an engine for internal failure?

4. What function does the spectrometric oil analysis engine inspection program perform?

5. What is the purpose of the turbine condition monitoring program?

6. What should always be checked before starting to work on a reciprocating engine involving turning the propeller?

7. During an engine removal, what precautions or checks need to be done with regard to the fuel valves and the battery or electrical systems?

8. On nose wheel aircraft, when removing the engine, what type of precaution needs to be taken with regard to the aircraft's stability?

9. What precautions should be taken when removing and storing fluid lines and hoses?

10. What should the propeller be checked for before ground operation?

Chapter 8, Section B - Engine Removal and Replacement

Name:_____ Date:_____

PAGE LEFT BLANK INTENTIONALLY

Section C
Final Chapter Exam

1. If metallic particles are found in the oil filter during an inspection _____
   ☐ A. it is an indication of normal engine wear unless the particles are nonferrous.
   ☐ B. the cause should be identified and corrected before the aircraft is released for flight.
   ☐ C. it is an indication of normal engine wear unless the deposit exceeds a specified amount.

2. A characteristic of dyna focal engine mounts as applied to aircraft reciprocating engines is that the _____
   ☐ A. shock mounts eliminate the torsional flexing of the powerplant.
   ☐ B. engine attaches to the shock mounts at the engine's center of gravity.
   ☐ C. shock mounts point toward the engine's center of gravity.

3. During routine inspection of a reciprocating engine, a deposit of small, bright, non-magnetic metallic particles is discovered in the oil sump and on the surface of the oil filter. This _____
   ☐ A. may be a result of abnormal plain type bearing wear and is cause for further investigation.
   ☐ B. is probably a result of ring and cylinder wall wear and is cause for engine removal and/or overhaul.
   ☐ C. is normal in engines utilizing plain type bearings and aluminum pistons and is not cause for alarm.

4. What is the purpose of a power check on a reciprocating engine?
   ☐ A. To check magneto drop.
   ☐ B. To determine satisfactory performance.
   ☐ C. To determine if the fuel/air mixture is adequate.

5. Who establishes the recommended operating Time Between Overhauls (TBO) of turbine engines used in general aviation?
   ☐ A. The engine manufacturer.
   ☐ B. The operator (utilizing manufacturer data and trend analysis) working in conjunction with the FAA.
   ☐ C. The FAA.

6. On a reciprocating engine aircraft using a shrouded exhaust muffler system as a source for cabin heat, the exhaust system should be _____
   ☐ A. visually inspected for any indication of cracks or a operational carbon monoxide detection test should be done.
   ☐ B. replaced at each reciprocating engine overhaul by a new or overhauled exhaust system or an hydrostatic test should be accomplished.
   ☐ C. removed and the exhaust muffler checked for cracks by using magnetic particle inspection method or an hydrostatic test should be done on the exhaust muffler.

7. Bonding jumpers should be designed and installed in such a manner that they _____
   ☐ A. are not subjected to flexing by relative motion of airframe or engine components.
   ☐ B. provide a low electrical resistance in the ground circuit.
   ☐ C. prevent buildup of static electrical charge between the airframe and the surrounding atmosphere.

8. Which statement is true regarding proper throttle rigging of an airplane?
   ☐ A. The throttle stop on the carburetor must be contacted before the stop in the cockpit.
   ☐ B. The stop in the cock pit must contacted before the stop on the carburetor.
   ☐ C. The throttle control is properly adjusted when neither stop makes contact.

9. How often should float carburetors be overhauled?
   ☐ A. At engine overhaul.
   ☐ B. Annually.
   ☐ C. At engine change.

10. What type of nuts are used to hold exhaust systems to the cylinders?
   ☐ A. Brass or heat resistant nuts.
   ☐ B. High-temperature fiber self locking nuts.
   ☐ C. High-temperature aluminum self locking nuts.

ENGINE REMOVAL AND REPLACEMENT

11. Self-locking nuts may be used on aircraft provided that _____
    - ☐ A. the bolt and nut are safety wired.
    - ☐ B. the bolt and nut are not under tension.
    - ☐ C. the bolt or nut is not subject to rotation.

12. Aircraft bolts with a cross or asterisk marked on the bolt head are _____
    - ☐ A. made of aluminum alloy.
    - ☐ B. close tolerance bolts.
    - ☐ C. standard steel bolts.

13. After repairing an engine mount by welding, why is it considered good practice to normalize a part after welding?
    - ☐ A. To relieve internal stresses developed within the base metal.
    - ☐ B. To increase the hardness of the weld.
    - ☐ C. To remove the surface scale formed during welding.

14. The replacement of a damaged engine mount with a new identical engine mount purchased from the aircraft manufacturer is considered a _____
    - ☐ A. major or minor repair, depending upon the complexity of the installation.
    - ☐ B. major repair.
    - ☐ C. minor repair.

15. What does TBO stand for _____
    - ☐ A. Time Before Oil.
    - ☐ B. Time Before Overhaul.
    - ☐ C. Typical Buildup Oil.

16. Engine operational problems can be reason to overhaul an engine if which of the following is occurring?
    - ☐ A. Excessive engine vibration.
    - ☐ B. High magneto RPM drop.
    - ☐ C. Low engine time.

17. Before installing an engine, a careful inspection should be made of _____
    - ☐ A. Ignition switch.
    - ☐ B. the engine mount.
    - ☐ C. fuel tank.

18. If the engine is removed due to an internal failure, what should be inspected?
    - ☐ A. Any component that comes into contact with the oil system.
    - ☐ B. Magneto for failure.
    - ☐ C. Carburetor for failure.

19. Before installing metal tubing with threaded fittings ensure the threads are _____
    - ☐ A. very course.
    - ☐ B. preoiled.
    - ☐ C. clean.

20. All engine controls must be accurately adjusted to ensure _____
    - ☐ A. instantaneous response and stop to stop travel.
    - ☐ B. they completely close only.
    - ☐ C. they stay open.

21. Before an engine can be started for the first time after installation or overhaul it must be _____
    - ☐ A. it must be turned up to speed.
    - ☐ B. primed with fuel in the main bearings.
    - ☐ C. it must be or should be preoiled.

22. The propeller should be checked for _____
  - ☐ A. correct safety on bolts.
  - ☐ B. proper torque on mounting bolts.
  - ☐ C. both A and B.

23. After the engine has been ground run-up adjustments may be needed to _____
  - ☐ A. gas tank cleaned.
  - ☐ B. ignition timing and oil pressure setting.
  - ☐ C. removed engine mounts and checked.

24. On a turbofan engine installation the engine mount functions to _____
  - ☐ A. completely stop all vibration transmitted to the airframe structure.
  - ☐ B. open the after burner in flight.
  - ☐ C. support the engine on the ground and in flight and transmit loads to the aircraft structure.

25. Dehydrator plugs are blue when they are _____
  - ☐ A. ready to use.
  - ☐ B. full of moisture.
  - ☐ C. ready to reheat.

ENGINE REMOVAL AND REPLACEMENT

PAGE LEFT BLANK INTENTIONALLY

Section A
Study Aid Questions - Fill In The Blanks

1. Several general failures or hazards can result in _____ or _____ peculiar to turbine engine aircraft because of their operating characteristics.

2. A complete fire protection system includes both a _____ and a _____ system.

3. Two common engine fire detection systems used are _____ and _____ systems.

4. _____ systems use individual sensors to monitor a fire zone.

5. _____ systems provide more complete fire detection coverage by using several loop type of sensors.

6. _____ are heat-sensitive units that complete electrical circuits at a certain temperature.

7. The _____ is constructed of two dissimilar metals, such as chromel and constantan.

8. A _____ depends on the rate of temperature rise and does not give a warning when an engine slowly overheats or a short circuit develops.

9. Optical sensors often referred to as "flame detectors", are designed to alarm when they detect the presence of specific _____ from _____ flames.

10. Pneumatic detectors are based on the principles of _____ .

11. A _____ permits more complete coverage of a fire hazard area than any of the spot-type temperature detectors.

12. Two widely used types of continuous-loop systems are the _____ and the _____ systems.

ENGINE FIRE PROTECTION SYSTEMS

13. The _____ system uses a slender inconel tube packed with thermally sensitive eutectic salt and a nickel wire center conductor.

14. _____ systems are two complete basic fire detection systems with their output signals connected so that both must signal to result in a fire warning.

15. The fixed fire extinguisher systems used in most engine fire protection systems are designed to dilute the atmosphere with an _____ that does not support _____.

Section A
True of False

_____ 1. A cartridge (squib) and frangible disk type valve on fire extinguisher containers are installed in the outlet of the discharge valve assembly.

_____ 2. A combination gauge switch visually indicates actual container pressure and also provides an electrical signal if container pressure is lost.

_____ 3. The fenwal system also has a temperature compensated pressure switch that tracks the container pressure variations with temperatures by using a hermetically sealed reference chamber.

_____ 4. Discharge indicators provide immediate visual evidence of container over pressure indication on fire extinguishing systems.

_____ 5. The thermal discharge indicator is connected to the fire container relief fitting and ejects a red disk to show when container contents have dumped overboard due to excessive heat.

_____ 6. If the flight crew activates the fire extinguisher system, a yellow disk is ejected from the skin of the aircraft fuselage.

_____ 7. Fire switches are typically installed on the center overhead panel or center console in the flight deck.

_____ 8. The distance between clamps on straight runs, usually about 18–28 inches, is specified by the manufacturer.

_____ 9. Kinks and sharp bends in the sensing element of a fire detection system can cause an internal wire to short intermittently to the outer tubing.

_____ 10. Fire extinguisher containers are checked periodically to determine that the pressure is between the prescribed minimum and maximum limits.

Section A
Matching

Match the items numbered in the drawing to the terms below:

_____ Gland Nut   _____ Squib

_____ Bottle   _____ Electrical Connector

_____ Diaphragm   _____ Ground Lug

_____ Discharge Port

Match the items numbered in the drawing to the terms below:

_____ Safety Relief and Fill Port

_____ Identification Plate

_____ Squib

_____ Discharge Port

_____ Discharge Assembly

_____ Pressure Switch

_____ Handle

_____ Mounting Lug

_____ Pressure Switch Electrical Connector

_____ Pressure Switch and Test Button

ENGINE FIRE PROTECTION SYSTEMS

PAGE LEFT BLANK INTENTIONALLY

Section B
Knowledge Application Questions

1. What are the two major turbine failure modes as it pertains to overheat or fire conditions?

    1.   2.

2. Where are detectors placed to detect fires?

3. How do thermal switch units operate to indicate a fire?

4. Explain the operation of a pneumatic thermal fire detection system.

5. Explain the operation Fenwal continuous-loop fire detection system.

6. List the powerplant fire ZONES.

7. What is a HRD discharge system?

8. What would happen if a fire extinguisher container is exposed to excessive temperatures?

9. What type of indicator is used to show the fire container has been discharged because of a thermal over temperature?

10. Why should continuous-loop fire detection systems be inspected for kinks and sharp bends?

Chapter 9, Section B - Engine Fire Protection Systems

Name:_____ Date:_____

PAGE LEFT BLANK INTENTIONALLY

Section C
Final Chapter Exam

1. In a fixed fire extinguishing system, there are two small lines running from the system and exiting overboard. These line exit ports are covered with a blowout type indicator disc. Which one of the following statements is true?
   - ☐ A. When the red indicator disc is missing, it indicates the fire extinguishing system has been normally discharged.
   - ☐ B. When the yellow indicator disc is missing, it indicates the fire extinguishing system has been normally discharged.
   - ☐ C. When the green indicator disc is missing, it indicates the fire extinguishing system has had a thermal discharge.

2. Which of the following fire detection systems measures temperature rise compared to a reference temperature?
   - ☐ A. Thermocouple.
   - ☐ B. Thermal switch.
   - ☐ C. Lindberg continuous element.

3. How are most aircraft turbine engine fire extinguishing systems activated?
   - ☐ A. Electrically discharged cartridges.
   - ☐ B. Manual remote control valve.
   - ☐ C. Pushrod assembly.

4. Which of the following is the safest fire extinguishing agent to use from a standpoint of toxicity and corrosion hazards?
   - ☐ A. Dibromodifluoromethane (Halon 1202).
   - ☐ B. Bromochlorodifluoromethane (Halon 1211).
   - ☐ C. Bromotrifluoromethane (Halon 1301).

5. The explosive cartridge in the discharge valve of a fire extinguisher container is _____
   - ☐ A. a life dated unit.
   - ☐ B. not a life dated unit.
   - ☐ C. mechanically fired.

6. A fire detection system operates on the principle of a buildup of gas pressure within a tube proportional to temperature. Which of the following systems does this statement define?
   - ☐ A. Kidde continuous-loop system.
   - ☐ B. Pneumatic thermal fire detection system.
   - ☐ C. Thermal switch system.

7. How is the fire extinguishing agent distributed in the engine section?
   - ☐ A. Spray nozzles and fluid pumps.
   - ☐ B. Nitrogen pressure and slinger rings.
   - ☐ C. Spray nozzles and perforated tubing.

8. What is the principle of operation of the continuous-loop fire detector system sensor?
   - ☐ A. Fuse material which melts at high temperatures.
   - ☐ B. Core resistance material which prevents current flow at normal temperatures.
   - ☐ C. A bimetallic thermoswitch which closes when heated to a high temperature.

9. The fire detection system using a single wire surrounded by a continuous string of ceramic beads in a tube is the _____
   - ☐ A. fenwal system.
   - ☐ B. kidde system.
   - ☐ C. thermocouple system.

10. The fire detection system that uses two wires embedded in a ceramic core within a tube is the _____
    - ☐ A. fenwal system.
    - ☐ B. lindberg system.
    - ☐ C. kidde system.

ENGINE FIRE PROTECTION SYSTEMS

11. What is the function of a fire detection system?
    - ☐ A. To discharge the powerplant fire extinguishing system at the origin of the fire.
    - ☐ B. To activate a warning device in the event of a powerplant fire.
    - ☐ C. To identify the location of a powerplant fire.

12. What retains the fire extinguishing agent in a high rate of discharge (HRD) container?
    - ☐ A. Breakable disk and fusible disk.
    - ☐ B. Pressure switch and check tee valve.
    - ☐ C. Pressure gauge and cartridge.

13. How are most aircraft turbine engine fire extinguishing systems activated?
    - ☐ A. Electrically discharged cartridges.
    - ☐ B. Manual remote-control valve.
    - ☐ C. Pushrod assembly.

14. Which of the following fire detection systems are commonly used in an engine nacelle?
    - ☐ A. Fire detection control unit.
    - ☐ B. Thermocouple detector.
    - ☐ C. Kidde continuous-loop.

15. What is the function of a fire detection system?
    - ☐ A. To discharge the powerplant fire-extinguishing system at the origin of the fire.
    - ☐ B. To activate a warning device in the event of a powerplant fire.
    - ☐ C. To identify the location of a powerplant fire.

16. (Refer to the Figure 9-18) If a portable fire extinguisher's pressure is successfully verified in the early morning when the ambient temperature is 30°F, what will be its status later in the day if the temperature reaches 75°F?
    - ☐ A. The extinguisher will continue to be functional.
    - ☐ B. The extinguisher will be overcharged.
    - ☐ C. The extinguisher will be undercharged.

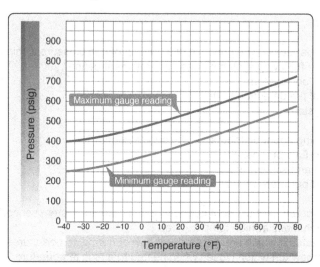

Figure 9-18. Fire extinguisher container pressure-temperature chart.

17. What retains the nitrogen charge and fire-extinguishing agent in a high rate of discharge (HRD) container?
    - ☐ A. Breakable disk and fusible disk.
    - ☐ B. Pressure switch and check tee valve.
    - ☐ C. Pressure gauge and cartridge.

18. Which of the following is NOT used to detect fires in reciprocating engine nacelles?
    - ☐ A. Smoke detectors.
    - ☐ B. Rate-of-temperature-rise detectors.
    - ☐ C. Flame detectors.

19. The most satisfactory extinguishing agent for a tailpipe or intake fire is _____
    - ☐ A. carbon dioxide.
    - ☐ B. dry chemical.
    - ☐ C. methyl bromide.

20. How is the fire-extinguishing agent distributed in the engine section?
    - ☐ A. Spray nozzles and fluid pumps.
    - ☐ B. Nitrogen pressure and slinger rings.
    - ☐ C. Spray nozzles and perforated tubing.

21. For fire detection and extinguishing purposes, aircraft powerplant areas are divided into fire zones based on _____
    - ☐ A. hot and cold sections of the engine.
    - ☐ B. the volume and smoothness of the airflow through engine compartments.
    - ☐ C. engine type and size.

22. Which of the following fire detection systems uses heat in the normal testing of the system?
    - ☐ A. The thermocouple system and the Lindberg system.
    - ☐ B. The Kidde system and the Fenwal system.
    - ☐ C. The thermocouple system and the Fenwal system.

23. The fire detection system that uses two wires embedded in a ceramic core within a tube is the _____
    - ☐ A. Fenwal system.
    - ☐ B. Lindberg system.
    - ☐ C. Kidde system.

24. The fire detection system that uses a single wire surrounded by a continuous string of ceramic beads in a tube is the _____
    - ☐ A. Fenwal system.
    - ☐ B. Kidde system.
    - ☐ C. thermocouple system.

25. The explosive cartridge in the discharge valve of a fire-extinguisher container is _____
    - ☐ A. a life-dated unit.
    - ☐ B. not a life-dated unit.
    - ☐ C. mechanically fired.

PAGE LEFT BLANK INTENTIONALLY

RECIPROCATING ENGINE
MAINTENANCE OPERATION

Section A
Study Aid Questions - Fill In The Blanks

1. Both maintenance and complete engine overhauls are performed normally at _____ .

2. A complete overhaul process will include the following ten steps:

    1. _____   6. _____

    2. _____   7. _____

    3. _____   8. _____

    4. _____   9. _____

    5. _____   10. _____

3. Major overhaul consists of the complete reconditioning of the powerplant as set forth in the ten step process of overhaul requiring that a reciprocating engine _____ be disassembled.

4. A _____ overhaul is not generally a _____ repair.

5. A certified powerplant rated technician can perform or supervise a major overhaul of an engine if it is not equipped with a(n) _____ or has a propeller reduction system other than _____ type gears.

6. The inspection of engine parts during overhaul is divided into three categories:

    1. _____   3. _____

    2. _____

7. When grit blasting all machined surfaces must be _____ properly and adequately, and all openings tightly _____ before blasting.

8. Magnetic particle inspection is a method of detecting invisible cracks and other defects in _____ such as iron and steel.

9. _____ can penetrate material and disclose discontinuities through the metal.

10. Dimensional inspection of the barrel consists of the following measurements:

1. _____   4. _____

2. _____   5. _____

3. _____

Section A
True of False

_____ 1. If an engine had a life of 2,000 hours and had been operated 500 hours it would have a TBO of 1,500 hours.

_____ 2. When dimensional tolerances are concerned, the manufacturer will publish a new, minimum and serviceable dimension for all critical component parts.

_____ 3. When dimensional tolerances are concerned, the technician must determine the serviceable dimension for all critical component parts.

_____ 4. A check of the engine's service bulletins, airworthiness directives, and type certificate compliance along with organizing the appropriate manuals, and reviewed the engine's history are all components of the receiving inspection.

_____ 5. Pitted surfaces in highly stressed areas resulting from corrosion can be removed and is cause of little concern.

_____ 6. While inspecting the cylinder head for internal and external cracks, use a bright light to inspect for cracks, and investigate any suspicious areas with a magnifying glass or microscope.

_____ 7. Regardless of the method and type of solution used, coat or spray all parts with lubricating oil immediately after cleaning to prevent corrosion.

_____ 8. The measurement for out-of-roundness is usually taken at the bottom of the cylinder only.

_____ 9. Deglazing the cylinder walls is accomplished with a valve seat grinding stone which causes, a crosshatch pattern on the cylinder wall to allow for piston ring break-in.

_____ 10. All measurements involving cylinder barrel diameters must be taken at a minimum of two positions 90° apart in the particular plane being measured.

Note the correct order for performing a penetrant inspection procedure.

_____ Drying the part.   _____ Applying the developer.

_____ Removing penetrant with remover   _____ Inspecting and interpreting results.
emulsifier or cleaner.

_____ Thorough cleaning of the metal surface.   _____ Applying penetrant.

Matching

Match the terms with the definitions:

Abrasion	Erosion	Inclusion	Cut	Stain
Brinelling	Flaking	Nick	Peening	Scoring
Burning	Fretting	Chafing	Pick Up/Scuffing	
Burnishing	Galling	Chipping	Pitting—Small	
Burr	Gouging	Corrosion	Upsetting	
Dent	Grooving	Crack	Scratches	

_____ 1. A small, rounded depression in a surface usually caused by the part being struck with a rounded object.

_____ 2. Loss of metal from the surface by mechanical action of foreign objects, such as grit or fine sand. The eroded area will be rough and may be lined in the direction in which the foreign material moved relative to the surface.

_____ 3. The breaking loose of small pieces of metal or coated surfaces, which is usually caused by defective plating or excessive loading.

_____ 4. A condition of surface erosion caused by minute movement between two parts usually clamped together with considerable unit pressure.

_____ 5. A severe condition of chafing or fretting in which a transfer of metal from one part to another occurs. It is usually caused by a slight movement of mated parts having limited relative motion and under high loads.

_____ 6. A furrowing condition in which a displacement of metal has occurred (a torn effect). It is usually caused by a piece of metal or foreign material between close moving parts.

_____ 7. A recess or channel with rounded and smooth edges usually caused by faulty alignment of parts.

_____ 8. Presence of foreign or extraneous material wholly within a portion of metal. Such material is introduced during the manufacture of rod, bar, or tubing by rolling or forging.

_____ 9. A sharp sided gouge or depression with a "V" shaped bottom which is generally the result of careless handling of tools and parts.

_____ 10. A series of blunt depressions in a surface.

_____ 11. A buildup or rolling of metal from one area to another, which is usually caused by insufficient lubrication, clearances, or foreign matter.

_____ 12. Hollows of irregular shape in the surface, usually caused by corrosion or minute mechanical chipping of surfaces.

_____ 13. A series of deep scratches caused by foreign particles between moving parts, or careless assembly or disassembly techniques.

_____ 14. Shallow, thin lines or marks, varying in degree of depth and width, caused by presence of fine foreign particles during operation or contact with other parts during handling.

_____ 15. A change in color, locally, causing a noticeably different appearance from the surrounding area.

_____ 16. A displacement of material beyond the normal contour or surface (a local bulge or bump). Usually indicates no metal loss.

RECIPROCATING ENGINE MAINTENANCE OPERATION

_____ 17. An area of roughened scratches or marks usually caused by foreign matter between moving parts or surfaces.

_____ 18. One or more indentations on bearing races usually caused by high static loads or application of force during installation or removal. Indentations are rounded or spherical due to the impression left by the contacting balls or rollers of the bearing.

_____ 19. Surface damage due to excessive heat. It is usually caused by improper fit, defective lubrication, or over temperature operation.

_____ 20. Polishing of one surface by sliding contact with a smooth, harder surface. Usually no displacement nor removal of metal.

_____ 21. A sharp or roughened projection of metal usually resulting from machine processing.

_____ 22. Describes a condition caused by a rubbing action between two parts under light pressure which results in wear.

_____ 23. The breaking away of pieces of material, which is usually caused by excessive stress concentration or careless handling.

_____ 24. Loss of metal by a chemical or electrochemical action. The corrosion products generally are easily removed by mechanical means. Iron rust is an example of corrosion.

_____ 25. A partial separation of material usually caused by vibration, overloading, internal stresses, defective assembly, or fatigue. Depth may be a few thousandths to the full thickness of the piece.

_____ 26. Loss of metal, usually to an appreciable depth over a relatively long and narrow area, by mechanical means, as would occur with the use of a saw blade, chisel or sharp-edged stone striking a glancing blow.

Chapter 10, Section A - Reciprocating Engine Maintenance Operation

Name:_____ Date:_____

Section B
Knowledge Application Questions

1. Explain what is meant by the term TBO as it pertains to aircraft engines.

2. Define a major overhaul.

3. Discuss why extreme care must be used if any water-mixed degreasing solutions containing caustic compounds or soap are used during the cleaning process.

4. With regard to magnetic particle inspection; an indication or discontinuity is present when?

5. Explain the procedure for clearing a liquid lock.

6. Define pre-ignition.

7. Define detonation.

8. Explain the use and purpose of a power check during the run-up procedure.

Chapter 10, Section B - Reciprocating Engine Maintenance Operation

Name:_____ Date:_____

PAGE LEFT BLANK INTENTIONALLY

Section C
Final Chapter Exam

1. If a radial engine has been shut down for more than 30 minutes, the propeller should be rotated through at least two revolutions to _____
   - ☐ A. check for hydraulic lock.
   - ☐ B. check for leaks.
   - ☐ C. prime the engine.

2. How is a flooded engine, equipped with a float-type carburetor, cleared of excessive fuel?
   - ☐ A. Crank the engine with the starter or by hand, with the mixture control in cutoff, ignition switch off, and the throttle fully open, until the fuel charge has been cleared.
   - ☐ B. Turn off the fuel and the ignition. Discontinue the starting attempt until the excess fuel has cleared.
   - ☐ C. Crank the engine with the starter or by hand, with the mixture control in cutoff, ignition switch on, and the throttle fully open, until the excess fuel has cleared or until the engine starts.

3. Priming of a fuel-injected horizontally opposed engine is accomplished by placing the fuel control lever in the _____
   - ☐ A. IDLE CUTOFF position.
   - ☐ B. AUTO RICH position.
   - ☐ C. FULL RICH position.

4. When first starting to move an aircraft while taxiing, it is important to _____
   - ☐ A. test the brakes.
   - ☐ B. closely monitor the instruments.
   - ☐ C. notify the control tower.

5. What may be used to check the stem on a poppet-type valve for stretch?
   - ☐ A. Dial indicator.
   - ☐ B. Micrometer.
   - ☐ C. Telescoping gauge.

6. Which tool can be used to measure the alignment of a rotor shaft or the plane of rotation of a disk?
   - ☐ A. Dial indicator.
   - ☐ B. Shaft gauge.
   - ☐ C. Protractor.

7. In magnetic particle inspection, a flaw that is perpendicular to the magnetic field flux lines generally causes _____
   - ☐ A. a large disruption in the magnetic field.
   - ☐ B. a minimal disruption in the magnetic field.
   - ☐ C. no disruption in the magnetic field.

8. One way a part may be demagnetized after magnetic particle inspection is by _____
   - ☐ A. subjecting the part to high voltage, low amperage ac.
   - ☐ B. slowly moving the part out of an ac magnetic field of sufficient strength.
   - ☐ C. slowly moving the part into an ac magnetic field of sufficient strength.

9. Generally, when an induction fire occurs during starting of a reciprocating engine, the first course of action should be to _____
   - ☐ A. discharge carbon dioxide from a fire extinguisher into the air intake of the engine.
   - ☐ B. continue cranking and start the engine if possible.
   - ☐ C. close the throttle.

10. Engine crankshaft runout is usually checked _____
    01. During engine overhaul.   03. After a prop strike or sudden engine stoppage.
    02. During annual inspection.   04. During 100-hour inspection.
    - ☐ A. 01, 03, and 04.
    - ☐ B. 01 and 03.
    - ☐ C. 01, 02 and 03.

RECIPROCATING ENGINE MAINTENANCE OPERATION

11. Excessive valve clearances will cause the duration of valve opening to _____
    - ☐ A. increase for both intake and exhaust valves.
    - ☐ B. decrease for both intake and exhaust valves.
    - ☐ C. decrease for intake valves and increase for exhaust valves.

12. Which of these conditions will cause an engine to have an increased tendency to detonate?
    01. High Manifold Pressure   03. Engine Overheat
    02. High Intake Air Temp.   04. Late Ignition Timing
    - ☐ A. 01, 04
    - ☐ B. 01, 02, 03
    - ☐ C. 01, 02, 03, 04

13. Which of the following would most likely cause a reciprocating engine to backfire through the induction system at low RPM operation?
    - ☐ A. Idle mixture too rich.
    - ☐ B. Clogged derichment valve.
    - ☐ C. Lean mixture.

14. Regarding the above statements:
    01. Pre-ignition is caused by improper ignition timing.
    02. Detonation occurs when an area of the combustion chamber becomes incandescent and ignites the fuel/air mixture in advance of normal timed ignition.
    - ☐ A. Only No. 01 is true.
    - ☐ B. Both No. 01 and No. 02 are true.
    - ☐ C. Neither No. 01 nor No. 02 is true.

15. If the ignition switch is moved from BOTH to either LEFT or RIGHT during an engine ground check, normal operation is usually indicated by a _____
    - ☐ A. large drop in RPM.
    - ☐ B. momentary interruption of both ignition systems.
    - ☐ C. slight drop in RPM.

16. One cause of after firing in an aircraft engine is _____
    - ☐ A. Sticking intake valves.
    - ☐ B. an excessively lean mixture.
    - ☐ C. an excessively rich mixture.

17. During overhaul, the disassembled parts of an engine are usually degreased with some form of mineral spirits solvent rather than water mixed degreasers primarily because _____
    - ☐ A. solvent degreasers are much more effective.
    - ☐ B. water mixed degreaser residues may cause engine oil contamination in the overhauled engine.
    - ☐ C. water mixed degreasers cause corrosion.

18. How is proper end-gap clearance on new piston rings assured during the overhaul of an engine?
    - ☐ A. Accurately measuring and matching the outside diameter of the rings with the inside diameter of the cylinders.
    - ☐ B. By using rings specified by the engine manufacturer.
    - ☐ C. By placing the rings in the cylinder and measuring the end-gap with a feeler gauge.

19. If the crankshaft runout readings are plus .002 inch and minus .003 inch, the runout is _____
    - ☐ A. .005 inch.
    - ☐ B. plus .001 inch.
    - ☐ C. minus .001 inch.

20. Grinding the valves of a reciprocating engine to a feather edge is likely to result in _____
    - ☐ A. Normal operation and long life.
    - ☐ B. Excessive valve clearance.
    - ☐ C. Pre-ignition and burned valves.

21. Who is responsible for making the entry in the maintenance records after an annual, 100 hour, or progressive inspection?
  ☐ A. The owner or operator of the aircraft.
  ☐ B. The person approving or disapproving for return to service.
  ☐ C. The designee or inspector representing the FAA Administrator.

22. A person installing a product, part, or appliance on a type certificated product must make certain that the item's records document what type of statement?
  ☐ A. The product, part, or material meets FAA airworthiness standards.
  ☐ B. A product produced by an owner or operator does not need a statement.
  ☐ C. The product or material was not produced under an FAA production approval.

23. Which maintenance record entry best describes the action taken for a control cable showing approximately 20 percent wear on several of the individual outer wires at a fairlead?
  ☐ A. Wear within acceptable limits, repair not necessary.
  ☐ B. Removed and replaced the control cable and re-rigged the system.
  ☐ C. Cable repositioned, worn area moved away from fairlead.

24. What is the means by which the FAA notifies aircraft owners and other interested persons of unsafe conditions and prescribes the condition under which the product may continue to be operated?
  ☐ A. Airworthiness Directives.
  ☐ B. Aviation Maintenance Alerts.
  ☐ C. Aviation Safety Data.

25. An FAA Form 337 is used to record and document _____
  ☐ A. preventive and unscheduled maintenance, and special inspections.
  ☐ B. major and minor repairs, and major and minor alterations.
  ☐ C. major repairs and major alterations.

Chapter 10, Final Chapter Exam - Reciprocating Engine Maintenance Operation

Name:_____ Date:_____

PAGE LEFT BLANK INTENTIONALLY

LIGHT SPORT AIRCRAFT ENGINES

Section A
Study Aid Questions - Fill In The Blanks

1. A Light Sport Aircraft (LSA) means an aircraft, other than a _____ or _____ that, since its original certification, has continued to meet the following:

    A. A maximum takeoff weight of not more than _____ (for aircraft not intended for operation on water; or _____ for an aircraft intended for operation on water.

    B. A maximum airspeed in level flight with maximum continuous power (Vh) of not more than _____ under standard atmospheric conditions at sea level.

    C. A maximum never-exceed speed (VNE) of not more than _____ for a glider.

    D. A single, _____ engine, if powered.

    E. A maximum seating capacity of no more than _____ , including the pilot.

    F. Fixed _____ , except for an aircraft intended for operation on water or a glider.

2. To be eligible for a repairman certificate LSA with an inspection rating, you must complete a _____ hour training course acceptable to the _____ on inspecting the particular _____ of experimental light sport aircraft for which you intend to exercise the privileges of this rating.

3. To be eligible for an LSA repairman certificate with a maintenance rating, you must complete a training course acceptable to the _____ on maintaining the particular class of _____ for which you intend to exercise the privileges of this rating. The training course must, at a minimum provide the following number of hours of instruction:

    A. For Airplane Class Privileges _____ Hours

    B. For Weight-Shift Control Aircraft Class Privileges _____ Hours

    C. For Powered Parachute Class Privileges _____ Hours

    D. For Lighter Than Air Class Privileges _____ Hours

    E. For Glider Class Privileges _____ Hours

LIGHT SPORT AIRCRAFT ENGINES

4. Three methods of cooling employed on various Rotax LSA engines are _____ , _____ , and _____ .

5. The _____ of the Rotax 914 is designed for liquid cooling of the cylinder heads and _____ cooling of the cylinders.

6. The three primary components of a Rotax 447 or 503 CDI ignition system are the _____ , two _____ , and an _____ .

7. The ROTAX 914 engine is provided with a _____ forced lubrication system.

8. The ROTAX 914 engine is equipped with a _____ unit which uses a breaker-less, _____ design, with an _____ .

9. The Jabiru 2200cc Aircraft Engine is a _____ cylinder, _____ stroke horizontally opposed air cooled engine.

Section A
True of False

_____ 1. Aeromax Aviation produces a version of a 500 hp (Continuous Power) engine.

_____ 2. The 0-200-A/B is a four cylinder carbureted engine producing 100 brake horsepower and has a crankshaft speed of 2,750 RPM.

_____ 3. The Lycoming 233-LSA series is light and capable of running on unleaded automotive fuels as well as aviation gasoline.

_____ 4. It is advisable to check the oil level prior to an oil change as it provides information about oil dilution and contamination.

_____ 5. Replacement of the oil filter and the oil change should be accomplished slowly to allow draining of the oil system and the hydraulic tappets.

_____ 6. Compressed air must not be used to blow through the oil system.

_____ 7. After the oil change is accomplished, the engine should be cranked by hand in the direction of engine rotation (approx. 20 turns) to completely refill the entire oil circuit.

_____ 8. Cleaning the oil tank is mandatory and requires venting of the oil system.

_____ 9. Remove the magnetic plug and inspect it for accumulation of metal chips.

_____ 10. Any quantity of metal chips found on the magnetic plug on a two cycle engine's crankcase requires, at a minimum, that the engine be disassembled and inspected.

_____ 11. Drain any water from fuel tank sump and/or water trap (if fitted).

_____ 12. As part of the daily maintenance checks, verify the coolant level in the overflow bottle and the security of the cap.

_____ 13. If the maximum admissible exhaust gas temperature is exceeded, reduce the engine power setting to the minimum necessary and carry out a precautionary landing.

_____ 14. If the engine is not going to be used for an extended period of time, certain measures must be taken to protect the engine against heat, direct sun light, corrosion and the formation of residues.

_____ 15. When plugs are removed from a warm engine, the inspection of the tip of the spark plug is of little use to indicate the health of the engine.

Matching

1. Identify each component with the proper term below:

A. Pressure Line   C. Oil Line   E. Oil Circuit Vent Bore
B. Oil Tank   D. Oil Cooler

1. _____   4. _____

2. _____   5. _____

3. _____

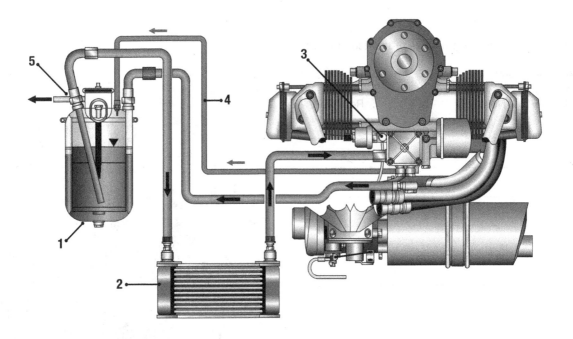

LIGHT SPORT AIRCRAFT ENGINES

2. Identify each component with the proper term below:

A. Return Spring   D. Throttle Lever
B. Adjustment Screw   E. Cable Fixation
C. Idle Adjustment   F. Carburetor Idle Stop

1. _____   4. _____

2. _____   5. _____

3. _____   6. _____

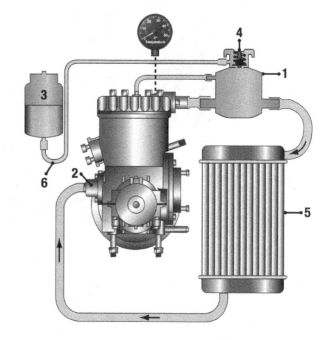

3. Identify each component with the proper term below:

A. Water Pump   D. Expansion Tank
B. Radiator   E. Pressure Valve
C. Overflow Hose   F. Reservoir

1. _____

2. _____

3. _____

4. _____

5. _____

6. _____

Chapter 11, Section A - Light Sport Aircraft Engines

Name:_____   Date:_____

Section B
Knowledge Application Questions

1. What is one very important characteristic of Light Sport Aircraft and Ultralight engines?

2. What is the definition of a powered parachute?

3. To be eligible for a repairman certificate with an inspection rating (Light Sport Aircraft) you must:

   1. _____

   2. _____

   3. _____

4. Explain the procedure for checking the friction torque in free rotation of the gear box.

PAGE LEFT BLANK INTENTIONALLY

Section C
Final Chapter Exam

1. Powered parachute means a powered aircraft comprised of _____
   ☐ A. a flexible or semi-rigid wing connected to a fuselage so that the wing is not in position for flight until the aircraft is in motion. the fuselage of a powered parachute contains the aircraft engine, a seat for each occupant and is attached to the aircraft's landing gear.
   ☐ B. a flexible or semi-rigid wing connected to a fuselage with a rotax engine.
   ☐ C. a powered parachute contains the fuselage, the aircraft engine, a seat for each occupant and is attached to the aircraft's landing gear.

2. One consideration when selecting a light sport engine is the shape and size and number of cylinders of the engine. Since these engines range from single cylinder to multi-cylinder engines, is the mounting in the airframe important to maintain _____
   ☐ A. the view of the pilot, aircraft center of gravity, and to increase aircraft drag.
   ☐ B. the view of the pilot, aircraft center of gravity, and to reduced aircraft drag.
   ☐ C. the view of the instruments, aircraft center of gravity, and to reduced aircraft drag.

3. To be eligible for a repairman certificate (Light Sport Aircraft) you must _____
   ☐ A. be at least 16 years old.
   ☐ B. be able to read, and write, and understand English. If for medical reasons you cannot meet one of these requirements, the FAA may place limits on your repairman certificate necessary to safely perform the actions authorized by the certificate and rating. Citizen of the United States, or similar residency status.
   ☐ C. demonstrate the requisite skill to determine whether a light sport aircraft is in a condition for safe operation.

4. To be eligible for a repairman certificate (Light Sport Aircraft) with an inspection rating, you must _____
   ☐ A. complete a 16-hour training course acceptable to the FAA on inspecting the particular class of experimental Light Sport Aircraft for which you intend to exercise the privileges of this rating.
   ☐ B. complete a 12-hour training course acceptable to the FAA on inspecting the particular class of experimental Light Sport Aircraft for which you intend to exercise the privileges of this rating.
   ☐ C. complete a 10-hour training course acceptable to the FAA on inspecting the particular class of experimental Light Sport Aircraft for which you intend to exercise the privileges of this rating.

5. Engine cooling for the Rotax 582 is accomplished by _____
   ☐ A. air cooled only.
   ☐ B. liquid cooled cylinders and cylinder heads along with air cooling.
   ☐ C. liquid cooled only.

6. The Rotax 912/914 engine uses a _____
   ☐ A. dry sump–forced lubrication system.
   ☐ B. wet sump-forced lubrication system.
   ☐ C. gravity lubrication system.

7. The HKS700T engine has _____
   ☐ A. 4 cylinders.
   ☐ B. 6 cylinders.
   ☐ C. 2 cylinders.

8. The Jabiru Light sport engine uses _____
   ☐ A. a direct crankshaft driven propeller.
   ☐ B. a reduction gear box.
   ☐ C. pulleys and belts for reduction.

9. The Rotax R912 ignition system receives its original operating power from _____
   ☐ A. the battery.
   ☐ B. charging coils in the generator.
   ☐ C. ignition coils.

10. What are some of the first items to check when troubleshooting a light sport engine?
   ☐ A. Oil level.
   ☐ B. Fuel and spark.
   ☐ C. Carburetor adjustments.

11. A light sport aircraft engine is can a considered reliable when it can perform _____
   ☐ A. cruise speed.
   ☐ B. specified rating.
   ☐ C. Climb performance.

12. How many people including the pilot can a light sport aircraft carry?
   ☐ A. 2
   ☐ B. 3
   ☐ C. 4

13. The TBO varies with each manufacturer, but is dependent on _____
   ☐ A. maintenance received.
   ☐ B. time at high power settings.
   ☐ C. both A and B.

14. How is the Rotax 912/914 4 cylinder opposed engine cooled?
   ☐ A. Air cooled only.
   ☐ B. Air cooled and liquid cooled.
   ☐ C. Liquid cooled only.

15. The Rotax 914 is provided with what type of lubrication system?
   ☐ A. Wet sump.
   ☐ B. Combination wet and dry.
   ☐ C. Dry sump.

16. The Jabiru light sport engine is made with _____
   ☐ A. a propeller direct drive and crankshaft driven.
   ☐ B. has a reduction gear box.
   ☐ C. has two reduction gear boxes.

17. The Jabiru 3300 engine features _____
   ☐ A. 100 hp and 4 cylinders.
   ☐ B. 120 hp and 6 cylinders.
   ☐ C. 90 hp and 2 cylinders.

18. The Great Plains aircraft VW conversion engine is a _____
   ☐ A. 4 cycle 4 cylinder.
   ☐ B. 4cycle 2 cylinders.
   ☐ C. 2 cycle 4 cylinders.

19. How many carburetors does a 912/914 Rotax engine have?
   ☐ A. One
   ☐ B. Three
   ☐ C. Two

20. Teledyne Continental 0-200 A/B produces _____
   ☐ A. 80 hp at 2100 rpm.
   ☐ B. 100 hp at 2750 rpm.
   ☐ C. 100 hp at 2100 rpm.

21. The Lycoming 0-233 light sport engine is a _____
   ☐ A. experimental non-certified engine.
   ☐ B. certified engine.
   ☐ C. certified experimental engine.

22. If a light sport aircraft engine knocks under load, what is the probable cause?
    ☐ A. Induction system leak.
    ☐ B. The fuel/air mixture is too lean.
    ☐ C. Octane rating of fuel is too low.

23. When checking oil level on a 914 Rotax engine, _____
    ☐ A. make sure the engine is hot.
    ☐ B. turn the propeller several times by hand in the direction of engine rotation until it pumps all the oil from the engines oil tank.
    ☐ C. turn the propeller several times by hand against the direction of engine rotation until it pumps all the oil to the engines oil tank.

24. When the magnetic plug is removed and you are looking at the end of it what does that show _____
    ☐ A. oil level.
    ☐ B. metal chips accumulating on the plug.
    ☐ C. type of oil in the engine.

25. When troubleshooting an engine problem, it is most likely to fall into _____
    ☐ A. fuel and ignition system problems.
    ☐ B. oil system problems and magnetic plugs.
    ☐ C. cooling systems and baffling.

Chapter 11, Final Chapter Exam - Light Sport Aircraft Engines

Name:_____   Date:_____

PAGE LEFT BLANK INTENTIONALLY

CHAPTER 1
Aircraft Engines

Section A - Fill in the Blanks
1. Atmospheric air; rocket
2. fuel flow; (lbs./hr.); thrust; brake horsepower
3. crankcase
4. Excessive vibration; wear rapidly
5. compression
6. tapered, splined, or flanged
7. force; distance
8. Thrust horsepower
9. function; simultaneously
10. average pressure; combustion chamber; indicated horsepower
11. percentages
12. cylinders; total piston displacement of the engine
13. 59°F. or 15°C; 14.69 lbs. / sq. in; 29.92
14. turbofan, turboprop, turboshaft, turbojet
15. centrifugal flow and axial flow

Section A - True or False
1. True	5. False	9. True
2. False	6. True	10. True
3. True	7. True	11. True
4. True	8. False	12. True

Section A - Matching
A - Exhaust Valve	I - Push Rods
F - Intake Valve	N - Valve Guides
J - Piston	D - Valve Seats
B - Connecting Rod	M - Valve Springs
H - Rocker Arm	G - Rocker Arm Shaft

Section B - Knowledge Application
1. By displacing air opposite to the direction in which the aircraft is propelled, thrust is developed. This is an application of Newton's third law of motion.
2. Compression rings prevent the escape of combustion gases past the piston during engine operation. They are placed in the ring grooves immediately below the piston head. Most aircraft engines use two compression rings plus one or more oil control rings.
3. The opposed-type engine has two banks of cylinders directly opposite each other with a crankshaft in the center. It is generally mounted with the cylinders in a horizontal position. The opposed-type engine has a low weight-to-horsepower ratio, and its narrow silhouette makes it ideal for a horizontal installation.
4. When the engine valve is closed, the face of the tappet body (cam follower) is on the base circle or back of the cam. The light plunger spring lifts the hydraulic plunger so that its outer end contacts the push rod socket, exerting a light pressure against it. As the plunger moves outward, the ball check valve moves off its seat. Oil from the supply chamber, which is connected with the engine lubrication system, flows in and fills the pressure chamber. As the camshaft rotates, the cam pushes the tappet body and the hydraulic lifter outward. This forces the ball check valve onto its seat; thus, the body of oil trapped in the pressure chamber acts as a cushion. When the engine valve is off its seat, a predetermined leakage occurs between plunger and cylinder bore which compensates for any expansion or contraction in the valve train. When the valve closes, the amount of oil required to fill the pressure chamber flows in from the supply chamber, preparing for another cycle.
5. Indicated horsepower = PLANK / 33,000: Where: P = Indicated mean effective pressure in psi; L = Length of the stroke in ft. or in fractions of a foot; A = Area of the piston head or cross-section of the cylinder, in sq. in.; N = Number of power strokes per minute; RPM.; K = Number of cylinders.
6. An air inlet; Compressor section; Combustion section; Turbine section; Exhaust section; Accessory section; Auxiliary systems such as starting, lubrication, fuel supply, and auxiliary purposes, such as anti-icing, cooling, and pressurization.
7. F = M × A Where F = Force in pounds; M = Mass in lbs in per seconds; A = Acceleration in ft. per sec. per sec. In the above formula "mass" is similar to "weight," but it is actually a different quantity. Mass refers to the quantity of matter, while weight refers to the pull of gravity on that quantity. At sea level under standard conditions, 1 lb. of mass will have a weight of 1 lb. To calculate the acceleration of a given mass, the gravitational constant is used as a unit of comparison. The force of gravity is 32.2 ft./sec.2 (or feet per second squared). This means that a free-falling 1-lb., object will accelerate at the rate of 32.2 feet per second each second that gravity acts on it. Since the object mass weighs 1 lb., which is also the actual force imparted to it by gravity, we can assume that a force of 1 lb. will accelerate a 1-1 object at the rate of 32.2 ft./sec. 2.
8. The ratio of net work produced by the engine to the chemical energy supplied in the form of fuel.
9. Many turbine blades are cast as a single crystal which gives the blades better strength and heat properties. Heat barrier coating such as ceramic coating and air flow cooling help keep the turbine blades and inlet nozzles cooler. This allows the exhaust temperature to be raised increasing the efficiency of the engine.
10. The centrifugal-flow compressor consists basically of an impeller (rotor), a diffuser (stator), and a compressor manifold, . Centrifugal compressors have a high pressure rise per stage which can be around 8:1. Generally centrifugal compressors are limited to two stages due to efficiency concerns.

ANSWERS

CHAPTER 2
Engine and Fuel Metering Systems

Section A - Fill in the Blanks
1. fuel; fuel metering device
2. AVGAS; Jet-A
3. red; blue
4. schedule (meter)
5. low lead; lead
6. electronic sensors; computer logic
7. parameters; on-board computer
8. High; low
9. Vapor lock
10. dropping; increased
11. induction system icing; vaporization
12. Acceleration
13. fuel economy; richer
14. cylinder head; intake port
15. atomize; vaporize

Section A - True or False
1. True	5. True	9. True	13. True
2. True	6. False	10. False	14. False
3. True	7. False	11. False	15. True
4. False	8. True	12. True	

Section A - Matching
1. Fuel Inlet Screen
2. Mixture Control
3. Economizer
4. Idling System
5. Throttle Valve
6. Venturi
7. Main Discharge Nozzle
8. Main Air Bleed
9. Main Metering Jet
10. Accelerating Pump
11. Float
12. Needle Valve
13. Float Chamber

Section B - Knowledge Application
1. Transfer of heat from the engine tends to cause boiling of the fuel in the lines and the pump. This tendency is increased if the fuel in the tank is warm. High fuel temperatures often combine with low pressure to increase vapor formation.
2. The basic parts of a fuel system include tanks, boost pumps, lines, selector valves, strainers, engine-driven pumps, and pressure gauges.
3. It must meter fuel proportionately to air to establish the proper fuel/air mixture ratio for the engine at all speeds/altitudes which the engine may operate.
4. The carburetor uses a venturi to measure the airflow through the induction system and this measurement to regulate the amount of fuel discharged into the airstream.
5. The mixture control determines the ratio of fuel to air in the engine. With a cockpit control, the best mixture ratio can be set to suit operating conditions.
6. Because of the decrease in air temperature resulting from the evaporation of fuel introduced into the airstream. As the fuel evaporates the temperature is lowered in the area were the evaporation takes place.
7. The level of fuel in the chamber is kept nearly constant by means of a float-operated needle valve and a seat.
8. Less danger of induction icing as the temperature drop due to vaporization takes place in or near cylinder. Acceleration is improved due to the positive action of the injection system. Injection improves fuel distribution reducing overheating of individual cylinders caused by variation in mixture. Gives better fuel economy than a carburetor in which the mixture to most cylinders must be richer than necessary so that the cylinder with the leanest mixture will operate properly.
9. Connect and adjust carburetor or throttle controls so full movement of the throttle is obtained with full movement of the control in the cockpit. Check and adjust the throttle linkages so spring back on the throttle quadrant is equal in both the "full open" and "full closed" positions. Correct any excess play or looseness of control. Controls should be checked so that they go stop to stop on the carburetor.
10. The result is incomplete combustion within the engine cylinder, with resultant formation of carbon deposits on the spark plugs and subsequent spark plug fouling.

CHAPTER 3
Induction and Exhaust Systems

Section A - Fill in the Blanks
1. air-scoop; inlet filter
2. air filter; dirt; foreign matter
3. updraft; downdraft
4. temperature; heat; dangerous icing zones.
5. airflow; manifold pressure
6. clouds, fog, rain, sleet, snow, clear air
7. cracks; leaks; security of mounting.
8. surpercharged; 30; ground boosted
9. fuel vaporization; hot; volumetric efficiency; detonation
10. exhaust gases; turbine; impeller
11. impeller; diffuser; casing
12. "backed up"; turbine wheel
13. fully open; overboard
14. engine oil
15. oil pressure
16. critical altitude; "full throttle"
17. differential pressure controller
18. Inlet Guide Vanes (IGV)
19. inlet screens; FOD
20. test stand; moves

Section A - True or False
1. True	5. True	9. True	13. True
2. False	6. True	10. True	14. True
3. False	7. False	11. False	15. False
4. True	8. True	12. False	

Section A - Matching
1. Exhaust Manifold
2. Engine Oil Pressure Inlet or Waste Gate Actuator

3. Differential Pressure Control
4. Density Controller
5. Exhaust Bypass Valve Assembly or Waste Gate
6. Exhaust Gas Discharge
7. Turbocharger
8. Filter
9. Air Inlet

Section B - Knowledge Application

1. It provides optimum airflow to each cylinder throughout a wide operational range. Air from the induction manifold flows into the intake ports where it is mixed with fuel from the fuel nozzles and then enters the cylinders as a combustible mixture as the intake valve opens.

2. Induction ice can be prevented or eliminated by raising the temperature of the air that passes through the system, using a carburetor heat system located upstream near the induction system inlet and well ahead of the dangerous icing zones.

3. When the throttle is placed in a partly closed position, it limits the amount of air available to the engine. When the aircraft is in a glide a fixed-pitch propeller windmills causing the engine to consume more air than it normally would at this same throttle setting, thus adding to the lack of air behind the throttle. The partly closed throttle, establishing a higher than normal air velocity past the throttle, and an extremely low pressure area is produced. This lowers the air temperature surrounding the throttle valve. If the temperature in this air falls below freezing and moisture is present, ice will form on the throttles and nearby units restricting the air flow to the engine causing it to quit.

4. A true supercharged engine can boost the manifold pressure above 30 inches of mercury and are called ground boosted. In other words a true supercharger will boost the manifold pressure above ambient pressure.

5. Externally driven superchargers derive their power from the energy of engine exhaust gases directed against a turbine that drives an impeller that compresses the incoming air.

6. The position of the waste gate valve, which determines power output, is controlled by oil pressure. Engine oil pressure acts on a piston in the waste gate assembly which is connected by linkage to the waste gate valve.

7. The pressure and temperature sensing bellows of the density controller react to changes between the fuel-injector inlet and the turbocharger compressor. The bellows, filled with dry nitrogen, maintains a constant density by allowing the pressure to increase as the temperature increases.

8. Movement of the bellows repositions the bleed valve, causing a change in the quantity of bleed oil, which changes the oil pressure on top of the waste gate piston. The differential pressure controller functions during all positions of the waste gate valve other than the "fully open" position

9. The inlet must be able to recover as much of the total pressure of the free airstream as possible. As air molecules are trapped and begin to be compressed in the inlet much of the pressure loss is recovered. This added pressure at the inlet of the engine increases the pressure and air flow to the engine. This is known as "ram recovery" or, sometimes, as "total pressure recovery".

10. When the velocity at the nozzle opening becomes Mach 1, the flow will only pass at this speed. If there is sufficient flow to maintain Mach 1 at the nozzle opening and have extra flow (flow that is being restricted by the opening), this is termed a choked nozzle. The extra flow will build up pressure in the nozzle which is sometimes called pressure thrust.

CHAPTER 4
Ignition and Electrical Systems

Section A - Fill in the Blanks

1. magneto-ignition; electronic Full Authority Digital Engine Control (FADEC)
2. Dual magnetos
3. high-tension magneto
4. permanent magnet; current
5. engine; proper stroke; crankshaft degrees; position
6. magnetic; primary; secondary
7. magnet; soft iron core; pole shoes
8. full register; magnetic
9. neutral position
10. pivotless;
11. secondary windings; coil; distributor rotor; distributor cap; ignition lead; spark plug
12. closed; magnetic lines; electromotive force
13. stopped; collapses
14. thousands; secondary; high; secondary circuit
15. Moisture

Section A - True or False

1. True	4. True	7. True	10. False
2. False	5. False	8. True	
3. True	6. True	9. False	

Section A - Matching

1. Adjusting Screw
2. Cam
3. P-Lead Terminal
4. Rubbing Block
5. Contact Points

9-High Output Coil	5-Cam
7-Distributor Block	6-Capacitor
1-Impulse Coupling	4-Ball Bearing
3-Pinion Gear	8-Distributor Gear
2-Magnet	

Section B - Knowledge Application

1. The function of this starting vibrator is to change the DC of the battery into a pulsating DC and deliver it to the primary coil of the magneto. The starting vibrator does not produce the high ignition voltage within itself.

ANSWERS

2. The function of the spark plug in an ignition system is to conduct a short impulse of high-voltage current through the wall of the combustion chamber.

3. Spark plugs operate at extreme temperatures, electrical pressures, and cylinder pressures. A cylinder operating at 2,100 RPM must produce approximately 17 distinct high-voltage sparks that bridge the air gap of a spark plug each second. The spark plug is subjected to temperatures over 3,000°F , gas pressures as high as 2,000 pounds per square inch (psi) and electrical pressure as high as 20,000 volts.

4. The three main components of a spark plug are the electrode, insulator, and outer shell.

5. The heat range of a spark plug is a measure of its ability to transfer the heat of combustion to the cylinder head. The plug must operate hot enough to burn off carbon deposits yet remain cool enough to prevent a pre-ignition condition.

6. The spark plug reach is the length of the threaded portion that is inserted in the spark plug bushing of the cylinder.

7. If ignition occurs too early, the piston rising in the cylinder is opposed by the full force of combustion. This condition results in a loss of engine power, overheating, and possible detonation and pre-ignition.

8. Top dead center is a piston and crankshaft position from which all other piston and crankshaft locations are referenced. When a piston is in the top dead center position of the crankshaft, it is also in the center of the no-travel zone.

9. The piston is in a position where a straight line can be drawn through the center of the crankshaft journal, the crankpin and the piston pin. Bench timing the magneto, or setting the E-gap, involves positioning the magneto rotor at the E-gap position and setting the breaker points to open when the timing lines or marks provided for that purpose are perfectly aligned.

10. After reaching the engine RPM specified for the ignition system check, allow the RPM to stabilize. Place the ignition switch in the right position and note the RPM drop on the tachometer. Return the switch to the both position. Allow the switch to remain in the both position for a few seconds so that the RPM stabilizes again. Place the ignition switch in the left position and again note the RPM drop. Return the ignition switch to the both position.

CHAPTER 5
Starting Systems

Section A - Fill in the Blanks
1. starting process.
2. Turbine
3. Air turbine; turbine wheel; compressors
4. reciprocating engines
5. turbine engines; air turbine
6. time limits; high energy
7. 1 minute; 1 minute; 1 minute; 5 minutes
8. starter solenoid
9. high pressure compressor
10. gas turbine; air
11. self-sustaining speed.
12. ignition; fuel
13. self-accelerating speed
14. axial flow turbine; reduction gear; starter clutch
15. volume; pressure

Section A - True or False
1. False	4. False	7. False	10. True
2. True	5. True	8. False	
3. True	6. True	9. True	

Section A - Matching
1. D	4. J	7. I	10. G
2. H	5. F	8. E	
3. C	6. A	9. B	

Section B - Knowledge Application
1. Turbine engine starters have a critical role to play in the starting of the engine. If for whatever the reason, the starter is not up for the task of turning the turbine engine up to a self sustaining speed the engine start process will not be successful.

2. The typical starter motor is a 12- or 24-volt, series-wound motor, which develops high starting torque.

3. In a typical high-horsepower reciprocating engine starting system, the direct-cranking electric starter consists of two basic components: a motor assembly and a gear section. The gear section is bolted to the drive end of the motor to form a complete unit.

4. A starter solenoid is activated by either a push button or turning the ignition key on the instrument panel. When the solenoid is activated, it's contacts close and electrical energy energizes the starter motor. Initial rotation of the starter motor engages the starter through an overrunning clutch in the starter adapter, which incorporates worm reduction gears.

5. It uses an electric motor and a drive gear that engages as the motor is energized and spins the gear which moves out and engages the ring gear on the propeller hub cranking the engine for start. As the engine starts, the starter drive gear is spun back by the engine turning which disengages the drive gear.

6. Hold a strip of double-0 sandpaper or a brush seating stone against the commutator as it is turned. The sandpaper or stone should be moved back and forth across the commutator to avoid wearing a groove. Roughness, out-of-roundness, or high-mica conditions are reasons for turning down the commutator.

7. At low cranking speeds, the fuel flow is not sufficient to enable the engine to accelerate, and so the starter continues to crank the engine until self-accelerating speed has been attained. If

assistance from the starter were cut off below the self-accelerating speed, the engine would either fail to reach idle speed, or might even decelerate because it could not produce sufficient energy to sustain rotation or to accelerate during the initial phase of the starting cycle. Due to low air flow this could also cause a hot start.

8. The air to operate an air turbine starter is supplied from either a ground-operated air cart the APU or a cross bleed start from an engine already operating.

9. When the bleed valve and start valve is open, the regulated air passing through the inlet housing of the starter impinges on the turbine, causing it to turn. As the turbine turns, the gear train is activated and the inboard clutch gear, which is threaded onto a helical screw, moves forward as it rotates and its jaw teeth engage those of the outboard clutch gear to drive the output shaft of the starter.

10. The air to operate an air turbine starter is supplied from either a ground-operated air cart the APU or a cross bleed start from an engine already operating.

CHAPTER 6
Engine Lubrication

Section A - Fill in the Blanks
1. friction; moving
2. Oil; lubrication
3. friction; energy; heat
4. Sliding friction; plain
5. rolling friction; ball; roller; anti-friction
6. Wiping friction; loads; extreme.
7. cooling; 50; cooling; heat; cooler
8. cushion
9. cleans; filter.
10. corrosion; coating; corrosion; rust; corrode.
11. cold temperatures; operating temperatures
12. viscosity index; viscosity
13. dry sump lubrication
14. bypass valve; clogged
15. Spectrometric oil analysis program

Section A - True or False
1. True	4. False	7. True	10. True
2. True	5. True	8. True	
3. False	6. False	9. False	

Section A - Matching
1. Iron	6. Silver
2. Chromium	7. Titanium
3. Aluminum	8. Molybdenum
4. Nickel	9. Phosphorous
5. Tin	10. Lead

Section B - Knowledge Application
1. In addition to reducing friction, the oil film acts as a cushion between metal parts. This cushioning effect is particularly important for such parts as reciprocating engine crankshaft and connecting rods, which are subject to shock-loading. The load bearing qualities of the oil prevent the oil film from being squeezed out allowing metal to metal contact in the bearing. Also as oil circulates through the engine, it absorbs heat from the pistons and cylinder. These components are especially dependent on the oil for cooling. Oil can account for up to 50% of the total engine cooling and is a great medium to transfer the heat from the engine to the oil cooler. The oil also aids in forming a seal between the piston and the cylinder wall to prevent leakage of the gases from the combustion chamber. Oils clean the engine by reducing abrasive wear by picking up foreign particles and carrying them to a filter. The dispersant (an additive) in the oil holds the particles in suspension and allows the filter to trap them as the oil passes through. Oil also prevents corrosion on the interior of the engine by leaving a coating of on parts when the engine is shut down.

2. Large engine operating clearances due to the relatively large size of the moving parts, the different materials used, and the different rates of expansion of the various materials; high operating temperatures and high bearing pressures.

3. Viscosity index indicates the effect of temperature changes on the viscosity of the oil. When oil has a low index it signifies a relatively large change of viscosity with changes of temperature. The oil becomes thin at high temperatures and thick at low temperatures. Oils with a high viscosity index will have small changes over a wide temperature range.

4. Positive introduction of oil to the bearings; Cooling effect caused by the large quantities of oil which can be (pumped) circulated through a bearing. Satisfactory lubrication of the engine components in various attitudes of flight.

5. An oil pressure regulating valve limits oil pressure to a predetermined value, depending on the installation. This valve is sometimes referred to as a relief valve but its real function is to regulate the oil pressure at a present pressure level.

6. As oil enters the gear chamber, it is "picked up" by the gear teeth, trapped between them and the sides of the gear chamber, and is carried around the outside of the gears and discharged from the pressure port into the oil screen passage.

7. Gasoline; Moisture; Acids; Dirt; Carbon; Metallic particles.

8. Check for premature or excessive engine component wear which will be indicated by the presence of metal particles, shavings, or flakes in the oil filter element or screens. The oil filter can be inspected by opening the filter paper element. Check the condition of the oil from the filter for signs of metal contamination. Remove the paper element from the filter and unfold the paper element for material trapped in the filter. If the engine employs a pressure screen, check the screen for metal particles. After draining the oil, remove the suction screen from the sump and check for metal particles.

9. Oil jets (or nozzles) are located in the pressure lines adjacent to, or within the bearing compartments

and rotor shaft couplings. Oil from these nozzles is delivered as an atomized spray. Some engines use an air-oil mist spray, which is produced by tapping high-pressure bleed-air from the compressor to the oil nozzle outlet. This method is adequate for ball and roller bearings; however, the solid oil spray is considered the better of the two methods.

10. The EGT indicator, consist of a thermocouple placed in the exhaust stream just after the cylinder port. It is then connected to the instrument in the panel. This allows for the adjustment of the mixture which will have a large effect on engine temperature.

CHAPTER 7
Propellers

Section A - Fill in the Blanks
1. RPM
2. engine
3. Slip; geometric; effective
4. Geometric
5. Effective
6. Centrifugal force
7. Torque bending
8. Thrust
9. Aerodynamic twisting
10. Centrifugal twisting
11. Fixed pitch
12. constant speed; throttle; mixture; blue
13. test club
14. oil pressure
15. under-speed condition
16. over-speed condition
17. on-speed
18. feathering
19. reversible pitch propeller
20. electrical propeller icing

Section A - True or False
1. True	4. False	7. True	10. False
2. True	5. True	8. True	
3. False	6. False	9. True	

Section A - Matching
1. Pilot Controls
2. Pilot Valve
3. Flyweights
4. Speeder Spring

1. Propeller Governor
2. Spider Hub
3. Servo Piston Dome
4. Feathering Spring
5. Blade Actuating Lever
6. Oil Transfer Sleeve

Section B - Knowledge Application
1. The work done by the thrust is equal to the thrust times the distance it moves the airplane (Work = Thrust × Distance). The power expended by the thrust is equal to the thrust times the velocity at which it moves the airplane (Power = Thrust × Velocity). If the power is measured in horsepower units, the power expended by the thrust is termed thrust horsepower.

2. A propeller must withstand severe stresses, which are greater near the hub, caused by centrifugal force and thrust.

3. Stresses increase in proportion to the RPM.

4. Tractor propellers are mounted on the upstream end of a drive shaft in front of the supporting structure. Most aircraft are equipped with this type of propeller. A major advantage of the tractor propeller is that lower stresses are induced in the propeller as it rotates in relatively undisturbed air.

5. The controllable-pitch propeller permits a change of blade pitch, or angle, while the propeller is rotating. This permits the propeller to assume a blade angle that will give the best performance for particular flight conditions.

6. A governor is an engine RPM sensing device and high pressure oil pump. In a constant speed propeller system, the governor responds to a change in engine RPM by directing or releasing oil under pressure to the propeller hydraulic cylinder. The change in oil volume in the hydraulic cylinder changes the blade angle and maintains the propeller system RPM. The governor is set for a specific RPM via the cockpit propeller control, which compresses or releases the governor speeder spring.

7. Most multiengine aircraft are equipped with propeller synchronization systems. Synchronization systems provide a means of controlling and synchronizing engine r.p.m. Synchronization reduces vibration and eliminates the unpleasant beat produced by unsynchronized propeller operation.

8. An auto feather system is used normally only during takeoff approach and landing. It is used to feather the propeller automatically if power is lost from either engine. The system uses a solenoid valve to dump oil pressure from the propeller cylinder (this allows the prop to feather) if two torque switches sense low torque from the engine. This system has a test/off/arm switch that is used to arm the system. Composite blades need to be visually inspected for nicks, gouges, loose material, erosion, cracks and debonds, and lightning strike. Composite blades are inspected for delaminations and debonds by tapping the blade or cuff (if applicable) with a metal coin.

9. Blade tracking is the process of determining the positions of the tips of the propeller blades relative to each other. (blades rotating in the same plane of rotation). Tracking shows only the relative position of the blades, not their actual path. The blades should all track one another as closely as possible. The difference in track at like points must not exceed the tolerance specified by the propeller manufacturer.

10. Balancing the propulsion assembly can provide substantial reductions in transmitted vibration and noise and also reduces excessive damage to other aircraft and engine components.

CHAPTER 8
Engine Removal and Replacement

Section A - Fill in the Blanks
1. operational use; manufacture; operation; maintenance
2. manufacturer; service
3. stoppage
4. engine seizure; propeller blades; one
5. Metal particles; failure
6. ferrous; magnetic
7. ferrous; concern
8. Spectrometric oil analysis program
9. Parts Per Million (PPM)
10. engine condition program
11. corrosion; freedom of operation
12. engine nacelle
13. bolts
14. security; cracks; excessive corrosion
15. ground check

Section A - True or False
1. True	4. True	7. False	10. True
2. True	5. True	8. True	
3. False	6. False	9. True	

Section A - Matching
26 Upper Shroud	16 Compressor Plenum
19 Bleed Air Flange	14 Bonding Jumper
24 Fuel Heater	6 Receptacle for the APU Harness
21 Hoist Assembly	
11 Electrical Plug for the APU Generator	13 Electrical Plug for the Generator Control
15 Cradle Base	4 Receptacle for APU Electrical Generator
2 Lock Handle	
8 Bleed Air Valve	10 Electrical Plug for the Starter Motor
27 EGT Receptacle	
25 Bleed Air Duct Coupling	7 Accessory Cooling Air Duct Flange
9 Engine Mount Bracket	5 Receptacle for Generator Control
23 Engine Mount Bracket and Vibration Isolator	3 Receptacle for Starter Motor
20 Fire Detection Sensor Element Receptacle	12 Electrical Plug for the APU Harness
22 Fire Extinguisher Line Fitting	1 Bleed Air Duct
18 EGT Plug	17 Bleed Load Control Air Line Fitting

Section B - Knowledge Application
1. Operational use, the quality of manufacture or overhaul, the type of aircraft in which it is installed, the kind of operation being carried out, and the quality of maintenance.
2. A rapid and complete stoppage of the engine caused by engine seizure or by one or more propeller blades striking an object so that RPM goes to zero in less than one revolution of the propeller.
3. Before removing an engine for suspected internal failure as indicated by foreign material on the oil screens or oil sump plugs, determine if the foreign particles are ferrous metal by placing them close to see if they are magnetic. If the material is not magnetic, it will not be attracted by the magnet. Any ferrous metal in the oil screens is cause for concern.
4. Spectrometric Oil Analysis allows an oil sample to be analyzed for the presence of minute metallic elements in parts per million (PPM). The analyzed elements are grouped into wear metals and additives and their measurement provides the data that analysts can to determine the engine's condition. An increase in PPM can signal component wear or pending failure of the engine. As samples are taken over time each amount of wear metals are recorded and noted.
5. Many turbine engines are monitored by an engine condition program which helps determine the health of the engine. This can also be called trend analysis, performance monitoring but it consist of mainly monitoring certain engine parameters generally daily and watching for trend shifts or changes in the engine parameters. If key parameters shift (change over time) this could be a warning that the engine has serious internal deterioration and should be overhauled.
6. Always be sure that the magneto switch is in the "OFF" position. Aircraft engines can be started accidentally by turning the propeller, if the magneto switch is on.
7. Check that all fuel selectors or solenoid-operated shutoff valves are closed. If solenoid-operated shutoff valves are installed, it may be necessary to turn the battery switch on before the valves can be closed. After ensuring that all fuel to the engine is shut off, disconnect the battery to eliminate the possibility of a "hot" wire starting a fire.
8. Be sure that the tail is supported so that the aircraft cannot tip back when the weight of the engine is removed from the forward end. Check the wheel chocks, if these are not in place, the aircraft can, and probably will, inch forward or back.
9. Some type of a container should be used to catch any fuel, oil, or other fluid that may drain from the disconnected lines. After the lines have drained, they should be immediately plugged or covered with moisture proof tape to prevent foreign matter from entering them as well as to prevent any accumulated fluid from dripping out.
10. The propeller, if equipped, must be checked before, during, and after the engine has been ground operated. The propeller should be checked for proper torque on the mounting bolts, leaks, vibration, and for correct safety.

ANSWERS

CHAPTER 9
Engine Fire Protection Systems

Section A - Fill in the Blanks
1. overheat conditions; fires
2. fire detection; extinguishing
3. spot detectors; continuous-loop
4. Spot detector
5. Continuous-loop
6. Thermal switches
7. thermocouple
8. thermocouple
9. radiation emissions; hydrocarbon
10. gas laws
11. continuous-loop detector
12. kidde; fenwal
13. fenwal
14. dual-loop
15. inert agent; combustion

Section A - True or False
1. True	4. False	7. True	10. True
2. True	5. True	8. False	
3. False	6. True	9. True	

Section A - Matching
3	Gland Nut	4	Squib
2	Bottle	7	Electrical Connector
1	Diaphragm	6	Ground Lug
5	Discharge Port		

10	Safety Relief and Fill Port	4	Pressure Switch and Test Button
8	Identification Plate	2	Pressure Switch
6	Squib	1	Handle
5	Discharge Port	9	Mounting Lug
7	Discharge Assembly	3	Pressure Switch Electrical Connector

Section B - Knowledge Application
1. The two major types of turbine failure can be classified as thermodynamic and mechanical.
2. To detect fires or overheat conditions, detectors are placed in the various fire zones to be monitored.
3. These thermal switches are heat-sensitive units that complete electrical circuits at a certain temperature. They are connected in parallel with each other, but in series with the indicator lights.
4. The sensing element consists of a closed helium-filled tube connected at one end to a responder assembly. As the element is heated, gas pressure inside the tube increases until the alarm threshold is reached. An internal switch then closes and reports an alarm to the cockpit.
5. The Fenwal system uses a slender inconel tube packed with thermally sensitive eutectic salt and a nickel wire center conductor. The control unit impresses a small voltage on the sensing elements. When an overheat condition occurs along the element length, the resistance of the eutectic salt within the sensing element drops sharply, causing

current to flow between the outer sheath and the center conductor. This current flow is produces a signal to actuate the output relay and fire alarm.
6. (1) the engine power section; (2) the engine accessory section; (3) except for reciprocating engines, any complete compartment in which no isolation is provided between the power section and accessory section; (4) any APU compartment; (5) any fuel-burning heater and other combustion equipment installation; (6) the compressor and accessory sections of turbine engines;(7) sections of turbine engine installations that contain lines or components carrying flammable fluids or gases.
7. High rate of discharge (HRD) systems use open-end tubes to deliver a quantity of extinguishing agent in 1-2 seconds.
8. Each container incorporates a temperature/pressure sensitive relief diaphragm that prevents container pressure from exceeding test pressure in the event of excessive temperatures.
9. The thermal discharge indicator is connected to the fire container relief fitting and ejects a red disk to show when its contents have dumped overboard due to excessive heat. The agent discharges through the opening created when the disk blows out giving flight and maintenance crews an indication that the extinguisher container needs to be replaced before the next flight.
10. Kinks and sharp bends in the sensing element can cause an internal wire to short intermittently to the outer tubing. The fault can be located by checking the sensing element with an ohm meter while tapping the element in the suspected areas to produce the short.

CHAPTER 10
Reciprocating Engine Maintenance Operation

Section A - Fill in the Blanks
1. Specified intervals
2. Receiving Inspection, Disassembly, Visual Inspection, Cleaning, Structural Inspection, NDT Inspection, Dimensional Inspection, Repair and Replacement, Reassembly, Testing and Break In.
3. crankcase
4. major, major
5. internal supercharger, spur
6. Visual, Structural (Nondestructive Testing, Dimensional
7. masked, plugged
8. ferromagnetic materials
9. X-rays
10. Maximum Taper of Cylinder Walls, Maximum Out of Roundness, Bore Diameter, Step, Fit Between Piston

Section A - True or False
1. True	5. False	9. False
2. True	6. True	10. True
3. False	7. True	
4. True	8. False	

Section A - Matching

1.	4	3.	1	5.	6
2.	3	4.	5	6.	2

1. Dent
2. Erosion
3. Flaking
4. Fretting
5. Galling
6. Gouging
7. Grooving
8. Inclusion
9. Nick
10. Peening
11. Pick up or Scuffing
12. Pitting - Small
13. Scoring
14. Scratches
15. Stain
16. Upsetting
17. Abrasion
18. Brinelling
19. Burning
20. Burnishing
21. Burr
22. Chafing
23. Chipping
24. Corrosion
25. Crack
26. Cut

Section B - Knowledge Application

1. Engine manufacturers set a total time in service in which the engine should be removed and overhauled. Overhaul time is in hours and referred to as time before overhaul (TBO). For example if an engine had a life of 2,000 hours and had run 500 its TBO would be 1,500.

2. Major overhaul consists of the complete reconditioning of the powerplant as set forth in the 10 step process. A reciprocating engine requires that the crankcase be disassembled.

3. These compounds are corrosive to aluminum and magnesium and may become impregnated in the pores of the metal and cause oil foaming when the engine is run. When using water mixed solutions, it is imperative that the parts be rinsed thoroughly in clear boiling water after degreasing.

4. Magnetic lines of force will be disturbed and opposite poles will exist on either side of the discontinuity. The magnetized particles thus form a pattern in the magnetic field between the opposite poles. This pattern, known as an "indication," assumes the approximate shape of the discontinuity.

5. Remove the front or rear spark plug of the lower cylinders and pull the propeller in the direction of rotation. The piston will expel any liquid present.

6. Pre-ignition means that combustion takes place within the cylinder before the timed spark jumps across the spark plug terminals. This condition can often be traced to excessive carbon or other deposits which cause local hot spots.

7. During normal combustion the flame fronts progress from the point of ignition across the cylinder, compressing the gases ahead of them. At the same time, the gases are being compressed by the upward movement of the piston. If the total compression on the remaining unburned gases exceeds the critical point, detonation occurs. Detonation is the spontaneous combustion of the unburned charge ahead of the flame fronts after ignition.

8. Specific RPM and manifold pressure relationship should be checked during the engine run-up in order to measure the performance of the engine against an established standard. Calibration tests have determined that the engine is capable of delivering a given power at a given RPM and manifold pressure. During the ground check, power is measured with the propeller. With constant air density, at any pitch position, will always require the same RPM to absorb the same horsepower.

CHAPTER 11
Light Sport Aircraft Engines

Section A - Fill in the Blanks

1. helicopter, powered lift
   1A. 1,320 pounds (600 kilograms; 1,430 pounds (650 kilograms)
   1B. 120 knots CAS
   1C. 120 knots CAS
   1D. reciprocating
   1E. two persons
   1F. landing gear
2. 16-hour, FAA, class
3. FAA, light sport aircraft
   3A. 120 hours
   3B. 104 hours
   3C. 104 hours
   3D. 80 hours
   3E. 80 hours
4. free air, fan colling, water colling
5. cooling system, ram-air
6. generator, charging coils, ignition capacitor
7. dry sump
8. dual ignition, capacitor discharge, integrated generator
9. 4 cylinder, 4 stroke

Section A - True or False

1.	False	5.	False	9.	True	13.	True
2.	True	6.	True	10.	False	14.	True
3.	True	7.	True	11.	True	15.	False
4.	False	8.	False	12.	False		

Section A - Matching

1-1. B	1-3. C	1-5. E
1-2. D	1-4. A	

2-1. D	2-3. F	2-5. A
2-2. B	2-4. E	2-6. C

3-1. D	3-3. F	3-5. B
3-2. A	3-4. E	3-6. C

Section B - Knowledge Application

1. Must be very light for the power they develop.
2. A powered aircraft comprised of a flexible or semirigid wing connected to a fuselage so that the wing is not in position for flight until the aircraft is in motion. The fuselage contains the engine, a seat for each occupant and is attached to the aircraft's landing gear.

ANSWERS

3. (A). Be at least 18 years old; able to read, speak, write, and understand English; (B). demonstrate the requisite skill to determine whether a light sport aircraft is in a condition for safe operation; (C). citizen of the United States, or a foreign country if lawfully admitted for permanent residence.

4. Fit the crankshaft with a locking pin. With the crankshaft locked, the propeller can be turned by hand 15 or 30 degrees depending on the dog gears installed. This is the maximum amount of movement allowed by the dog gears in the torsional shock absorption unit. (Ignition "OFF" and system grounded. Disconnect negative terminal of aircraft battery.) Turn the propeller by hand back and forth between ramps. No odd noises or irregular resistance must be noticeable during this movement. Attach a calibrated spring scale to the propeller at a certain distance (L) from the center of the propeller. Measure the force required to pull the propeller through the 15 or 30 degree range of free rotation. Calculate friction torque Newton meters (Nm) by multiplying the force Newton's (N) or pounds (lb) obtained on the spring scale by the distance the scale is attached from the center of the propeller (L). The distance measurement and torque measurement must be in the same units either standard or metric and cannot be mixed. The friction torque must be between 25 Nm and 60 Nm (18.5 to 44.3 ft-lb).